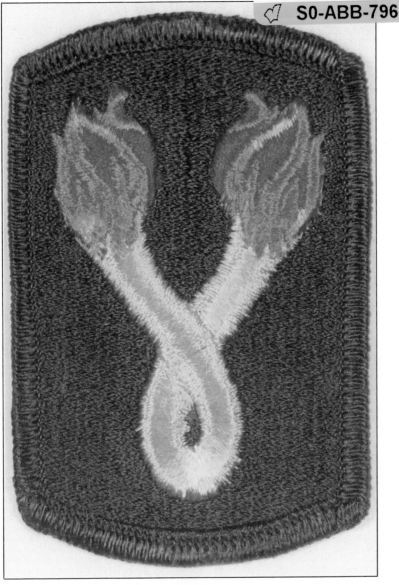

BANTAM BOOKS

TORONTO ● NEW YORK ● LONDON ● SYDNEY ● AUCKLAND

CHARGERS

by
F. Clifton Berry, Jr.

BLACK VIRGIN

The 196th's base camp at Tay Ninh and the looming shape of Nui Ba Den—the Black Virgin—wreathed in the mauve light of morning. Apart from its dominance of the landscape, the mountain provided the 196th Light Infantry Brigade with a unique vantage point—and the headache of keeping the Viet Cong out of the caves and tunnels below.

JUNCTION CITY

A convoy prepares to move out as members of the 4th Battalion, 31st Infantry, 196th Light Infantry Brigade, burn all logs and other materials used by the Viet Cong to build bunkers and other fortifications. This search-and-destroy action was part of Phase II of Operation Junction City, a large-scale sweep-and-clear operation in the spring of 1967 intended to drive the enemy from his strongholds.

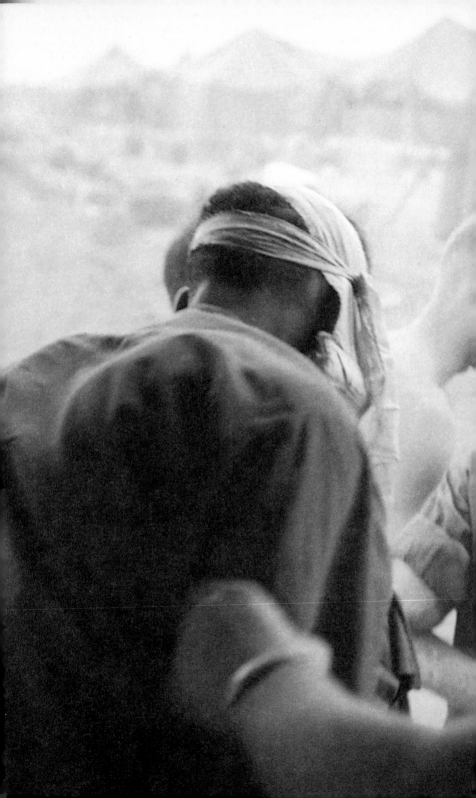

DUSTOFF

Medics of the 196th Light Infantry Brigade help wounded men from a medevac helicopter to a medical clearing station. At these stations casualties were sorted out as to seriousness and the type of wound to allow the worst cases to be evacuated first. Lightly wounded men were treated at the station while more serious cases eventually would be evacuated to the hospital at Chu Lai.

STILL WATERS

Men of Company C,
2d Battalion, 1st Infantry,
196th Light Infantry Brigade,
use a small boat as they search
huts along the Song An Tan River.
Regular patrols along this waterway with
its myriad tributaries in northern I Corps
implemented a policy of "active defense"
that denied the enemy a key supply route
and unearthed several arms caches.

POW CAMP

A military policeman with the 23rd Military Police Company, Americal Division, supervises Viet Cong prisoners of war (POWs) at the Americal Division collection camp at Chu Lai. The 196th, as one of the component brigades of the Americal Division, sent all prisoners to the collection point. There POWs had a choice of staying behind the wire or joining the Chieu Hoi (Open Arms) program and defecting to the side of the South Vietnamese government to work as Kit Carson Scouts with the US Army.

EDITOR IN CHIEF: Ian Ballantine. SERIES EDITORS: Richard Grant, Richard
Ballantine. PHOTO RESEARCH: John Moore. MAPS: Peter Williams.
PRODUCTION: Owen Watson. STUDIO: Kim Williams.
PRODUCED BY: The Up & Coming Publishing Company, Bearsville, New York.

CHARGERS
THE ILLUSTRATED HISTORY OF THE VIETNAM WAR
A Bantam Book/ June 1988

ACKNOWLEDGEMENTS
*This book is dedicated to the men who served in the 196th Light Infantry
Brigade. More than 1,000 died and 5,000 more were wounded. All were
changed by their service.*

*Photographs for this book were selected from the archives of DAVA,
Military Archive Research Services, and the personal collection of the author.
The diagram of LZ Mary Ann on page 140 is based on a sketch map
provided by Gary L. Knoller.*

Library of Congress Cataloging-in-Publication Data

Berry, F. Clifton.
    Chargers.

    (The Illustrated history of the Vietnam war)
    1. Vietnamese Conflict, 1961–1975—Regimental histories—United States.
2. United States. Army. Infantry Brigade, 196th—History. I. Title. II. Series.
DS558.4.B467   1988   959.704'342   87-47808
ISBN 0-553-34507-9

Published simultaneously in the United States and Canada

CW   0   9   8   7   6   5   4   3   2   1

replied okay. Carey looked up to see a sparkling thing coming at him.

"I screamed 'Grenade!' As I dropped down for cover, I saw it bounce off in the direction away from me and explode, *kaddaboom*. Again, twigs and dirt flew all over the place, but this time I was terrified."

The action built up at close quarters.

"Charlie was probing us. In turn, we were lobbing grenades and firing short bursts of covering fire."

One man was hit, not seriously, and the RTO called back to the company for advice. The patrol was told to stay put. Its location was plotted precisely. Supporting 105mm artillery fire would be laid around their position.

"A 105 round came breezing in and that was a real

Hostile country —A soldier examines the end of a piece of rope tied to strands of grass—a Viet Cong signal to warn villagers that the road had been mined.

kaddaboom, my first. The RTO proceeded to adjust the artillery. It's dark, there's shouting, the smell of gunpowder, shit flying all over the place. The incoming grenades seem to stop, when suddenly one 105 round comes in short, right on top of us. Doc lets out a blood-curdling scream: 'My leg, my leg!' How does one describe or outdo the word 'terrified'?"

The enemy kept firing. Carey and his buddies returned the fire, lobbed grenades, and held on.

"The RTO says he's hit, but not seriously. Pops (the 26-year-old) yells he's hit in the arm, somebody yells, 'Alabama's dead!'" Alabama was Carey's close buddy. They had linked up when they shipped out together from Oakland. "I go to pieces and break down. Doc continues to scream and scream (I didn't know he had morphine), while I'm crying and blubbering. I managed to keep some kind of control, only God knows how, and continued to fire short bursts. Only now I'm cursing Doc and praying at the same time for him to shut up, because he's giving away our position. I see another sparkling thing sailing toward us, *kaddaboom*. Crying, moaning, burntness, fumbling for another magazine for my M-16, please Doc cry quietly (his leg was blown off), muttering, sputtering, lobbed another grenade outward, saw a shadow move then scream as my grenade goes off . . . okay, now please go away, I'm sorry go away, get another magazine, search the moaning medic for his ammo, his grenades . . . the RTO says help is on the way, hang in there."

Help was on the way, but could the patrol hold out? Carey said, "Half crying, half sputtering, I yell, 'Please hurry, I'm low on ammo.' I see a shadow, I fire, it spins and disappears. I hear engine noises, big noises. It's tanks, tanks are coming, they're ours. I'm crying with relief. I hear noises out to my front, I fire another burst, them I'm out of ammo. Hurry tanks, please hurry. I hold the last grenade in my lap, whispering to Doc, 'Help is coming.' A lot of confusion, noises, lights. They're here. A bulldozer and two deuce and a half trucks; they're my tanks! A guy yells my name, 'I'm here.' Other guys are picking up Doc, a guy holds me up, says, 'It's okay, you're all right.' Ten of us walked out that night, six of us green. Four of us came back."

Richard Carey fought in many more small and large actions in his year in Vietnam, and survived.

FULL FIRE:
Barely a month in-country, a machine gunner and his assistant hose down a suspected enemy position during a search-and-destroy operation. The protective asbestos glove on the gunner's left hand was in case his M-60 overheated. Refinements like these, picked up in training, were soon discarded when they proved to be unnecessary encumbrances. Other lessons were learned the hard way; after a spell in-country, few risked firing at the enemy without taking cover.

But for him, as for most combat infantrymen, the first firefight remains forever vivid in his memory.

He was one of the new men who arrived at the 196th Brigade's Tay Ninh base camp between Christmas and New Year's. They came as individual replacements. The 196th's big combat in Operation Attleboro was a month in the past. It was fought by men who had been with the brigade more than a year. They came to Vietnam as members of integral units, a complete light infantry brigade, one-third of the combat power of a fighting division.

After his first combat, Richard Carey was no longer a greenseed. He was a blooded infantryman, part of a combat brigade whose units spent 2,200 days in Vietnam. The 196th Light Infantry Brigade was not the first into Vietnam, but it was the last one out. Its soldiers saw every kind of war in Vietnam from 1966 through 1972. Their war began when the unit arrived at Tay Ninh, west of Saigon, in mid-August 1966.

Black Virgin

Devens and Nui Ba Den

IT WAS mid-August 1966. A stream of C-130 Hercules transports was flying men of the 196th Light Infantry Brigade from the port of Vung Tau to the airstrip called Tay Ninh West.

Lieutenant Bob Duffey recalled his first sight of the 196th's new home. "I looked around and saw that great big mountain Nui Ba Den. And then I looked around some more and saw big wide-open fields with a couple of tents. I asked where the base camp was."

He was told, "That's it. You go build it." For the first couple of weeks in Vietnam, Duffey and 3,800 other soldiers of the 196th labored hard in the 95-degree heat of the southwest monsoon summertime, to the sound of pounding hammers, the buzz of chain saws, and the roar of bulldozer engines.

The base camp was a mixture of scrub brush and dry paddies. Anthills several feet high dotted the ground. The men worked day and night swinging hammers, shovels, machetes, and axes. They erected tents on wooden platforms, dug holes, filled sandbags, and strung communications wire.

When not building, they were training or preparing for combat. At night the men pulled security watches around the growing perimeter. The warm, humid darkness was often interrupted by the far-off glow of flares and the distant crackle of small arms fire. For the moment, the camp was quiet. But other American soldiers were fighting and dying nearby. Officers and men knew their turn would come soon enough.

Seven miles northeast, but seeming much closer, was a 3,235-foot mountain, Nui Ba Den (nicknamed the "Black Virgin"), which brooded over the camp. The first sight of Nui Ba Den is a shock. The

Black Virgin

FIRST IN: The first detachment of men of the 196th Infantry Brigade arriving at the Tay Ninh airstrip in August 1966. After a month's sea voyage from the States, they had landed at Vung Tau to the sounds of a band playing ''Sons of the Brave,'' and a welcoming party of 50 Vietnamese girls. They stuck flowers in the men's pockets, and on their packs and weapons as the band switched to ''Blue Hawaii.'' Then the troops boarded waiting C-130 transports to fly to Tay Ninh. The flower blossoms soon wilted, and the pleasantries of the welcome at Vung Tau faded into memory.

terrain around Tay Ninh, 50 miles northwest of Saigon near the Cambodian border, is flat for 40 miles in all directions, about 60 feet above sea level. The steep slopes of Nui Ba Den rise suddenly and precipitously, like a rockpile on a billiard table. In the rainy season the cloud base envelops the mountain halfway down by early afternoon. Even in the dry season, clouds often form near its summit.

The summit was a perfect observation post and radio relay site. Securing the relay station and the summit were two companies of Vietnamese irregulars (about 175 men), advised and directed by an officer and several sergeants of the US Special Forces.

However, the slopes and surrounding countryside were threatened by local and main-force units of the Viet Cong. Some units lived in tunnels and caves inside the huge rockpile. The mountain and nearby Tay Ninh City lay across the main routes of VC and North Vietnamese troops from their Cambodian sanctuary to the populous area around Saigon.

The main mission of the 196th Light Infantry Brigade was to find and fight those enemy units.

General William C. Westmoreland, US commander in Vietnam, put the 196th under control of the 25th Infantry Division, commanded by Maj. Gen. Frederick C. Weyand.

THE ORDERS activating the 196th had been read at Fort Devens, a few miles north and west of Boston, on 15 September 1965 by Colonel Frank S. Conaty. He had only a few officers and noncommissioned officers under his command, but thousands more were en route to Fort Devens.

The army was about to experiment, "train and retain." The 196th's nucleus of officers and noncoms would train recruits from scratch. Normally an outfit received men with basic and advanced individual training. But training centers such as forts Dix, Knox, Ord, and Jackson were running at full steam to fill units earmarked for deployment to Vietnam in 1966.

The experiment worked. Colonel Conaty was given a cadre of senior officers and noncoms with combat experience in World War II and Korea, and a sprinkling of juniors who had been advisors in the early days of Vietnam. A month after the activation, the

Founding commander —Col. Frank S. Conaty. In September 1965, Col. Conaty faced the challenge of creating a fighting infantry outfit from scratch, preparing it for combat, and getting ready to take it into battle. Conaty had met similar challenges before. He was a combat infantryman with experience in World War II and Korea. The new unit he was to create and command was designated the 196th Light Infantry Brigade.

Brand-new commander —Brig. Gen. Edward H. deSaussure, Jr., making a speech at the official welcoming ceremonies at Tay Ninh after the brigade's arrival in Vietnam shortly after he took over command. Under the rules then, a separate brigade rated a brigadier general at the top. A 1941 West Point graduate and career artilleryman, deSaussure had been an assistant division commander at the 25th Inf. Col. Frank Conaty, who built the brigade from scratch, remained as deputy commander.

new recruits came pouring in from the induction centers; about half were draftees, the others enlistees. Most had high school diplomas.

Halfway around the world, on 15 October, in the jungled hills of the Annamite Chain, the 2d Division of the North Vietnamese Army (NVA) was also being activated. Its main fighting forces were the 1st and 21st regiments. Five months later, infantry of the 3d NVA Regiment arrived from North Vietnam to become the third fighting regiment.

The 196th and 2d NVA Division were unaware of each other's preparations. However, the two units were destined to try to kill each other countless times in the years ahead.

Colonel Conaty and his cadre accepted men into units that had regular designations, such as 2d Battalion, 1st Infantry. After eight weeks' basic Army training, there followed advanced individual training, then unit and combat readiness training. The 196th was slated for the Dominican Republic.

The original complement was three infantry battalions, a jeep-mounted cavalry troop, and one artillery battalion of towed 105mm howitzers, with a support battalion, engineer and signal companies, and other supporting units. The 196th was the first of several such brigades: a light yet nearly self-sustained force.

Infantry battalions of the 196th were descendants of old-line regular Army units. 2d Battalion, 1st Infantry, traced its lineage back to March 1791. 3d Battalion, 21st Infantry, dated back to May 1861. 4th Battalion, 31st Infantry, went back to July 1916.

(Parent regiments are designated by a number and an arm of service, like 1st Infantry, 2d Cavalry, 82d Artillery. Subordinate battalions are linked with the parent regiment like this: 2d Bn, 1st Infantry. In conversation 3d Bn, 21st Infantry is called either "Three Two-One" or "Third of the Twenty-First." In military shorthand, it is written 3/21.)

Most unit training was done in the whistling winter winds of Camp Edwards on Cape Cod and in the deep snows of Camp Drum in northern New York. In spring 1966, units were finishing off the prescribed training cycle, including heavy emphasis on riot control in anticipation of the mission in the Dominican Republic.

By June, the new brigade was pronounced ready.

Plans for the move to Santo Domingo were completed on 23 June. Half the men were on pre-departure leave. But on June 24 the brigade received new orders: Prepare immediately for commitment to Vietnam.

All of the men returned from leave. Within three weeks, men and equipment were loaded aboard two transport ships, the USNS *Patch* and the USNS *Darby*, and sailed for Vietnam. The voyage took a month, enough time for the brigade's advance party to fly out to Vietnam, receive instructions, and lay plans for settling in at Tay Ninh.

Before the official welcoming ceremonies at Tay Ninh a couple of days later, General Westmoreland sent the 196th a new commander. A separate brigade then rated a brigadier general. So Brig. Gen. Edward H. deSaussure, Jr., one of Weyand's assistant division commanders at the 25th, was put in command. He was a 1941 graduate of West Point and a career artilleryman. Col. Frank Conaty, a veteran of World War II and Korea, remained as deputy commander.

THE PEACEKEEPERS: Men of the 196th practice riot control in training at Fort Devens. For many, the assignment to Vietnam came as a surprise. When the unit had been formed in September 1965, the 196th had been destined for peacekeeping duties in the Dominican Republic.

First in the field

Operations Attleboro, Cedar Falls, and Junction City

THE 3d BATTALION, 21st Infantry (nicknamed "Gimlets") went to the field first, on 2 September 1966. It started the search-and-destroy pattern of activity, aimed at disrupting enemy units and destroying their installations and supplies. Next in action was 4th Bn, 31st Infantry ("Polar Bears"), on 8 September.

After they returned, 2d Bn, 1st Infantry (2/1 Inf, commanded by Lt. Col. Charles "Pete" Weddle), went out into War Zone C. Its Company B killed a VC (Viet Cong) soldier first. It also had the first man of the 196th killed by the enemy, PFC Ron Taylor. This was the start of Operation Attleboro.

Only light contacts were made with enemy units during the first month. But officers and men gained experience in using supporting artillery fire, controlling helicopter assaults, and resupplying units by air. The infantry battalions rotated between base camp and jungle operations. Usually two battalions operated in the field, while one secured the base camp.

In mid-October, Phase II of Operation Attleboro was launched. Now the pace picked up. The aim was to search through a part of War Zone C east of Nui Ba Den and north of the large Michelin rubber plantations, believed to be one of the Viet Cong's largest storage and shipping areas. The task was to find the 9th VC Division's supply caches and concealed installations.

Weddle's 2/1 Infantry took to the field on 17 October. For the first few days, the enemy evaded contact. The infantrymen slogged through the double- and triple-canopy jungle in the muggy 95-degree heat. The search work was slow going, but they found plenty of evidence of enemy presence:

First in the field

TUNNEL SEARCH:

Armed with a flashlight, screwdriver, and pistol, a tunnel rat of the 196th squeezes through the trapdoor of a freshly discovered tunnel system. During operations Attleboro and Junction City, the 196th uncovered large sections of the Viet Cong tunnel network, but few Viet Cong. Every time US troops came close, the enemy used the interconnecting network of multilevel passages to make good their escape.

sampans, construction materials, ammunition, tunnels, and documents. One large hospital complex contained 27 structures above and below ground, with stores of medical supplies, clothing, rice, salt, canned milk, and peanuts.

Acting on intelligence information, General deSaussure ordered 2/1 Infantry to airlift a rifle company into a nearby area suspected of being a large VC supply dump. Company A flew into the landing zone on 29 October. Within four hours the troops uncovered more than 200 tons of rice, 440 gallons of gasoline, and 10 tons of salt.

The insignia of the 1st Bn, 27th Infantry —known as "The Wolfhounds."

The other companies of 2/1 Infantry flew into the site and immediately found tons of supplies concealed in the jungle. The enemy reaction was limited to harassing small arms fire. In four more days the 2/1 Infantry captured more than 820 tons of rice, 1,600 cans of milk, 25 tons of salt, and 1,200 pounds of fish, with smaller quantities of other supplies and equipment.

On 1 November, the 196th was ordered to expand the operation to brigade size. Its other two infantry battalions joined 2/1 Infantry in the jungle. An additional battalion from the 25th Division, 1st Bn, 27th Infantry, was put under 196th control. The "Wolfhounds" were welcome reinforcements, but at the same time, the 196th lost an essential man: Colonel Frank Conaty was transferred to command 1st Brigade, 25th Infantry Division.

Captured enemy documents showed that the enemy planned to take the Special Forces camp (at Soui Da), lure relief forces into ambush, and counterattack. The Third Corps "Mike Force" was dispatched to reinforce Soui Da on 2 November. The Americans organized 530 Nung tribesmen into three companies, led by a Special Forces officer and seven NCOs.

By 3 November, the Mike Force companies were patrolling north and east of Soui Da. South of them, the battalions of the reinforced 196th were beating the jungle, seeking the enemy.

On the morning of 3 November, the "Wolfhounds" were to be airlifted into a blocking position a few kilometers north of Weddle's 2/1 and Lt. Col. Hugh Lynch's 4/31 Infantry. If enemy forces withdrew ahead of Weddle's and Lynch's battalions, they would bump into the 1/27 Infantry. But the

COLD LZ:
Men of the 196th begin a sweep against the Viet Cong in War Zone C after being dropped into the landing zone (LZ) by brigade Hueys. An LZ was "cold" if it was unopposed by the enemy.

plan soon fell apart. Heavy contact was made and a fierce battle ensued.

Company B, 1/27 Infantry, flew into the landing zone (LZ) in two helicopter lifts. At 0922, the company commander reported, "LZ is cold." By 1018, the helicopters finished lifting Company C into the LZ and Company B was moving out to search the area. Eleven minutes later, enemy automatic weapons began firing at and hitting Company C.

Major Guy S. Meloy III commanded 1/27 Infantry. His Company C reported six men wounded, and more automatic weapons firing from a treeline. At 1050 Meloy called up helicopter gunships. He asked for air strikes, and alerted his Company A. By 1115 the gunships were striking the VC and Air Force

fighter-bombers added their weight of steel. Company C in the elephant grass continued to return enemy fire and take casualties. By 1145, Company C had lost 6 men killed, had 6 wounded, and its medics were running out of supplies. The VC held firm in fortified positions inside the heavy woods, firing prodigious bursts of machine gun and assault rifle fire. After another 20 minutes of fighting in the intense heat, Company C's commander was hit and its casualty list was up to 10 killed and 14 wounded. Meloy brought up his battalion logistics officer to take over Company C, ordered Company A airborne, and landed in Company C's hot spot.

A mile and a half southeast, the men of Pete Weddle's 2/1 Infantry started slogging through the

jungle to the aid of Meloy's battalion. It was slow, difficult hacking through the vines and clinging brush, knowing that VC were close by, in heavily fortified positions. In the fierce heat, the men became dehydrated. The brigade commander radioed messages to the battalion, urging it to hurry. The company's 2d Platoon, led by Lieutenant Perkins, pushed down two trails toward the firing. In their hurry they were bunched up closer than normal. A command-detonated Chinese claymore mine blew off its heavy charge. In one gigantic blast it cut down 24 men. From concealed bunkers and tree positions, a VC company opened up, pinning 2/1 Infantry down.

Further north the Mike Force hit a VC company that fired on them, disengaged, and withdrew northward.

General deSaussure airlifted Company C, 3/21 Infantry, into the action. Meloy ordered it into position on the right flank of his Company C. Meloy's battalion was still in heavy fighting, especially Company C. His men were running low on ammo. A resupply helicopter was shot down in the LZ. The VC fire was so intense that the Dustoff medevac helicopters could extract the wounded only when heavy smoke was laid and gunships roared in to shoot suppressive fire.

The volume of fire and types of weapons showed this was a main-force VC unit, part of the 9th VC Division. Meloy ordered his growing number of rifle companies to link up and dig in for the night. Two companies of 2/27 Infantry were pushed into the area to become a rapid reaction force.

Operation Attleboro had altered in a flash. From walks in the sun to find rice caches, it was developing into a major engagement with heavy casualties on both sides.

For the high command, this was an opportunity to fix and pound the 9th VC Division. To the infantrymen crawling through the bushes, it was grim death.

Lieutenant Bob Duffey's platoon of Company B, 2/1 Infantry, continued to cut methodically through the thick growth. They smacked up against an estimated VC company shooting small arms, automatic weapons, and blowing up heavy claymore antipersonnel mines. Duffey said, "It was physically

First in the field

PRAISE GOD AND PASS THE SALT: A PFC administers first aid to his buddy after he had collapsed from heat exhaustion during an operation. In the fierce, muggy 95-degree heat, the men quickly became dehydrated. Salt tablets soon became standard issue. During drawn-out encounters with the enemy it was not unusual for a company commander to call for a resupply of ammunition and salt tablets.

First in the field

JUNGLE WATCH: His M-16 at the ready, a PFC in the 196th watches for enemy activity during a search-and-destroy mission. The key to success in this sort of fighting was to keep moving. By constantly moving—albeit slowly and with difficulty through the heavy triple-canopy jungle, hacking through vines and clinging brush—the men of the 196th kept the enemy off balance.

impossible to move any faster through that jungle. The fighting was too spread out and too sporadic— it wasn't like there were clear-cut lines. You simply had to find the enemy and fight them where they were."

In the remaining hours of daylight, helicopters brought in fresh ammunition, water, and rations. That night was sleepless for most men. Although the enemy probed with grenades and automatic weapons, the troops stayed in their holes, holding fire to prevent revealing their positions.

The infantrymen spent the early morning hours preparing a coordinated attack. Had the enemy left the battlefield, or would he stay and fight? Soon after 1030 hours, the companies began moving, very slowly and carefully.

As Meloy's 1/27 moved slowly northeast, the lead men were hit with heavy automatic weapons fire from concealed positions. Helicopter gunships poured in suppressive fire, but the enemy blazed back at the gunships. By 1300 hours, Meloy's own Company A/1/27 was pinned down. On its left, Company C/3/21 Infantry was pinned down. Two companies of 2/1 Infantry were hacking through the jungle to reinforce. Meloy was wounded but still on his feet. Besides conducting the battle, he was calling for resupply of ammunition and salt tablets.

General deSaussure committed 2/27 Infantry to the relief of Meloy's 1/27 Infantry. By midafternoon on 4 November, Meloy's Company A had withstood three assaults by more than 100 VC each time. Casualties were mounting, but the fire was too intense for Dustoff medevac helicopters to lift out the wounded.

Company C/2/27 Infantry was coming to the relief of 1/27 Infantry. But it was quickly surrounded and cut off. At 1738 hours, Meloy radioed to Lt. Col. William C. Barott, commanding officer (CO) of 2/27 Inf, "I think we have VC between us."

Barott pushed forward to his Company A to lead an attack to link up with his cutoff Company C. He was killed, and Company C remained surrounded. Two attempts to reach the isolated Company C were only partially successful. Company A/2/1 Infantry found some men from Barott's Company C and carried them into their perimeter.

Company C/2/1 Infantry also attempted to reach

Double door —This enemy trap was one of many uncovered by the 196th during Operation Attleboro. It served as both an entrance to a tunnel network and a punji trap for US infantrymen. When not in use the entrance was covered with foliage that collapsed if anyone stepped on it. Just below surface level were spiked bamboo poles intended to impale the feet of the unsuspecting.

Metal probe —An SP4 probes in the mud for a possible Viet Cong mine after receiving a signal from his metal detector while sweeping a road in War Zone C. During Junction City the enemy frequently used mines and booby traps to avoid getting into major fights against the searching American infantrymen. On one occasion 24 men were cut down by the gigantic blast of a command-detonated Chinese claymore mine.

the cutoff company. Captain James P. Thompson moved his company forward through the dense jungle in complete darkness. They ran into a part of the 273d VC main force regiment. Enemy automatic weapons fire smashed into their flanks and front. Thompson tried to move one of his platoons to outflank the enemy, but it was also halted by murderous automatic weapons fire.

The remnants of C/2/27 were under command of a second lieutenant. Only 30 to 40 men remained effective. Meloy radioed, "We have made two attempts to reach their position and have suffered heavy casualties each time. They are about 150 meters north of my perimeter." So close, only one and one-half football fields. Yet so far, with strong VC units between.

All night, the enemy probed the companies dug into fighting holes. Meloy requested more ammunition and machine gun barrels for an early morning helicopter resupply.

That night the VC 272d Regiment (part of the 9th Division) attacked a nearby regional force outpost and mortared the 196th Brigade command post. The next morning a company of the Mike Force was overrun a few miles north.

Meloy attempted to reach the beleaguered Company C/2/27, but the enemy drove back every attempt. At 0925, he radioed, "They have us in a cross fire. Also receiving 60mm mortars." He called for air strikes with high-drag bombs and napalm to be brought in close. Companies from all three battalions were engaged around Meloy's core position, and the isolated Company C/2/27 was being ground down.

PFC John F. Baker, Jr., was at the head of Company A's column. With another man, he knocked out two bunkers. When his comrade was mortally wounded, Baker spotted the four VC who shot him and killed them. He led repeated assaults against enemy bunkers. One time an enemy grenade blew him off his feet. He got up, fighting mad. He destroyed one bunker, picked up a fallen machine gun, and charged another. He evacuated his wounded comrade and returned to the fight. When the unit was ordered to withdraw, he carried one wounded man to the rear, then raced back beyond friendly troops to attack and kill snipers harassing his unit.

When his ammunition was exhausted, he dragged two more wounded comrades to the rear. He justly earned the Medal of Honor for his extraordinary gallantry.

Now the VC concentrated on Meloy's command post and the companies around it. His reports over the radio tell the situation:

1000 hours: "The third try to get C/2/27 out we took quite a few casualties. This was another failure. Be advised there is a company-size VC element between 4/31 and myself with machine guns and automatic weapons."

1008: "We need more machine gun ammo, more morphine, and hand grenades."

1010: "We just had two company-size assaults. We beat both back."

1016: "Get a FAC in the air on my frequency."

1024: "We are under heavy contact again."

1026: Meloy called 4/31 Infantry, slogging toward him: "Come on in fast, we are in a big firefight." But 4/31 Infantry was itself tied up in a heavy fight.

Unofficial unit insignia —as it appeared on combat reports, bulletin boards, and in mess halls. To the men of the brigade, they were the Chargers. But to the brass they were the 196th Light Infantry Brigade. The title, "Light Infantry," referred to equipment, not numbers. The brigade numbered more than 6,000 men in three infantry battalions—a fighting force about one-third the size of a normal infantry division.

1030: "We are running out of people. We have had three major attacks this morning."

He recommended reinforcements be brought in. The FAC was overhead, and called for colored smoke to identify the friendly positions. 4/31 Infantry threw out yellow smoke, Meloy's companies popped green and violet. With the forward air controller (FAC) calling out locations by smoke, the 4/31 Infantry was able to head straight for Meloy. En route, they linked up with the pitifully small remnants of C/2/27.

This intense battle was raging in an area only about 2,000 yards in diameter. But the fight was hard to visualize because of the heavy double-canopy jungle, smoke from artillery and mortar explosions, gunfire, and general fog of battle.

Friendly companies trying to move toward each other kept encountering enemy machine guns in concealed concrete bunkers. By 1145, the situation was so confused that Meloy ordered all units to cease fire. Any firing would be VC.

While the 11 companies from 5 battalions were fighting for their lives, II Field Force alerted the 1st Infantry Division to take over the fight. Maj. Gen. William E. Depuy, commander of the "Big Red One," wasted no time. He was over the battlefield by noon and landed to confer with Meloy. The nearest airstrip was Dau Tieng, six miles south. Depuy started one of his battalions toward Dau Tieng immediately and alerted two brigades to assemble there as quickly as possible.

General Depuy decided to attack with fresh units on the next morning. The tired and battered soldiers who had fought hard for three days would be withdrawn.

As the afternoon wore on, the VC attacked Meloy's position and defended their bunkers. But heavy air strikes and artillery were poured in, and the 2/1 Infantry and 4/31 Infantry continued to press forward in the humid heat against intense enemy fire.

Companies A and B/3/21 Infantry secured the landing zone for extraction of Meloy's 1/27 Infantry and the remnants of 2/27 Infantry. At 1710, the extraction began; by 1758 the 1/27 and 2/27 were landing at Tay Ninh. There the battered battalions

ENEMY LOSSES AT ATTLEBORO

Killed	217
Prisoners	6
Structures	247
Tunnels	87
Bunkers	56
Punji pits	610
Trenches	52
Bridges	3
Base camps	6
Ammo	3,925
Mines	49
Grenades	229
Rockets	13
Rice	1,073 tons
Salt	25 tons
Fish	7,200
Peanuts	25,000 lbs
Rifles	22
Pistols	2

were put up in tents of the 196th units who remained on the battlefield. 2/1 Infantry held onto the field, although it had taken heavy casualties. (In B Company, nearly 100 of its 130 men had been hit.)

Wounded men were evacuated and replacements arrived. Lieutenant Bob Duffey recalled the grimmest task. "The hardest thing I had to do was identify so many of the dead in Operation Attleboro. It still gives me a lot of pain to remember their faces, the body bags, the tags tied to the toes and all that."

The 196th passed to control of the 1st Infantry Division on 6 November. General Depuy committed two brigades that morning. Higher headquarters soon committed the 173d Airborne Brigade and a brigade each of the 4th and 25th Infantry Divisions. Before long, 22,000 American soldiers were pitted against the 9th VC Division.

By 15 November the mauled 9th VC Division had yielded the field and slipped away into Cambodia.

General Westmoreland reported it left more than 1,100 dead.

The companies fought hard and well in toe-to-toe combat. But senior generals concluded that the 196th Brigade's command of the engagements fell short. General deSaussure was reassigned to a post at I Field Force Artillery.

General Westmoreland picked Brigadier General Richard T. Knowles to take immediate command, with authority to relieve all commanders. "We had a tremendous array of talent. The unit was well trained and responded instantly to new and inno-

First in the field

DOC:
A medic of B Co, 2d Bn, lst Inf, 196th Light Inf Bde, comforts a wounded man from his company who was hit by sniper fire during Operation Cedar Falls. The medics, trained in the essentials of field medicine, went out unarmed on patrol with units. This ability to dispense instant first aid to the wounded, often in the midst of combat, played a vital part in reducing battlefield mortalities.

vative ideas. Once the changes were made, everything fell into place. I had had the good fortune to have served in combat with several outstanding units (including the 1st Cavalry), and none were finer than the 196th."

In November and December, the 196th received replacements and continued combat operations in western Tay Ninh.

With the 9th VC Division withdrawn into Cambodia, Military Assistance Command Vietnam (MACV) wanted to put pressure on its redoubts closer to Saigon. The Iron Triangle, long a VC

NEW BROOM

Brig. Gen. Richard T. Knowles, appointed by General Westmoreland to take immediate command of the 196th after Operation Attleboro. Knowles was given authority to relieve all of the commanders in the 196th if necessary. He did not work that way. He said: "What I needed were the facts. I arrived, assumed command, was briefed on the situation, and went out to visit each major unit. It was my belief that in a situation like that one I had to start at the bottom and work up. The guys who had the most combat exposure were my prime concern."

Brig. Gen Richard T. Knowles

He visited all units and asked questions of the men, the noncommissioned officers, the lieutenants, and the company commanders. He found only a few weaknesses and shored them up quickly.

haven, was the target. A corps-sized operation, Cedar Falls, was laid on, using 1st and 25th Infantry Divisions (with the 196th attached), 173d Airborne Brigade, and 11th Armored Cavalry Regiment.

From start of Cedar Falls on 8 January to the end 17 days later, the US troops ground methodically through a maze of installations and tunnels. The enemy generally avoided contact.

Many of the 196th's troops became "tunnel rats." Sergeant Ronald Payne used a silencer-equipped revolver to shoot at VC troops who scurried through the tunnels ahead of him. Others used tear gas, plastic explosive, and smoke grenades to drive out the enemy, and destroy or deny the tunnel complexes to him. Knowles described one tunnel, more than 600 yards long with many side tunnels 16 feet underground, as a high-level headquarters that may have served the VC's 4th Military Region, including Saigon.

In November, December, and January, the brigade

lost three officers and 63 men killed; 11 officers and 222 men were wounded. Most casualties were suffered early in the period.

Operation Junction City would enter the virgin territory of War Zone C in force to trap and destroy VC and NVA units, and try to find the elusive COSVN, North Vietnam's overall headquarters for conducting the war.

The operation plan resembled a giant horseshoe, with the open end on the south and fighting units on east, north, and west. More than two-score battalions were sent to the field, including the three fighting infantry battalions of the 196th.

At sunrise on 22 February the deep red disk of the sun rose in the east past Nui Ba Den mountain, at the same time as the silvery circle of the full moon set in the west over the jungle. Hundreds of helicopters fluttered around Tay Ninh airstrip like swarms of dragonflies. They *wop-wopped* into columns, settled to the ground, and the troops piled aboard. Laden with weapons and ammunition, the men sweated heavily. The overnight temperature had gotten down only to 74 degrees.

Within minutes, the helicopters swarmed north. To the right, Nui Ba Den stood black and forbidding, with a doughnut ring of fog around its middle. En route to the LZs, the men could see the black teardrop scars of old napalm bursts, and the regularly spaced circles of B-52 strikes, half filled with green water.

The three battalions of Knowles's 196th assaulted three separate LZs that morning. Their LZs sealed off the northwest part of the area, along the Cambodian border. Other brigades of the 25th and 1st Infantry Divisions drove or helicoptered into position. Once most of the horseshoe was in place, a 778-man battalion task force of the 173d Airborne Brigade jumped into the northeast corner, and was soon reinforced by two more airborne battalions. Then the 11th Armored Cavalry Regiment and 2d Brigade, 25th Infantry Division, drove northward from the horseshoe's open end.

The 196th and other units spent the first weeks of Junction City sweating, humping, and searching the jungled redoubts, uncovering extensive supply caches and underground installations. Contact with enemy fighters was steady but moderate. COSVN

Wrong way up —Men of Battery C, 3d Bn, 82d Arty, 196th Light Inf Bde, push a cargo pack onto the correct side for unloading in War Zone C during the start of Operation Junction City. The operation to trap an increasingly elusive enemy depended on swiftness and surprise achieved by air-dropping men and equipment into the war zone.

First in the field

HANGING A ROUND: A PFC of D Co, 2d Bn, 1st Inf, 196th Inf Bde, hangs a round in an M-29 81mm mortar during Operation Cedar Falls. The 81mm mortar, capable of being rapidly field-assembled by three men, could generate a heavy volume of high-explosive fire in a matter of minutes. For the men of the 196th Light Infantry, for whom ''lightness'' was as much a mobile frame of mind as it was a matter of equipment, the mortar was an essential weapon. The 81mm was the second largest US infantry mortar and had an effective range of 3,500 meters.

Quick lift —A squad from Co B, 4th Bn, 31st Inf, 196th Light Inf Bde, wait to be airlifted by a UH-1D helicopter into a suspected enemy area during Junction City. The use of helicopters meant that troops could be rapidly redeployed as the circumstances dictated.

headquarters eluded detection, but the 196th found a psychological operations and propaganda outfit underground deep in the jungle, complete with printing presses, movie editing machines, and stocks of paper, ink, and film.

In the first phase of Junction City, which lasted until 5 March, the enemy avoided major fights. He used mines, booby traps, and small arms fire against the searching infantrymen. At night, VC mortars often slammed into US positions.

The key to success was to keep moving. By constantly moving, albeit slowly and with difficulty through the heavy jungle, platoons and companies kept the enemy off balance and moving in reaction. Units that stayed in place three days or more could expect to be hit with VC probes or mortar attacks. The VC needed a couple of days to fix the location of a US unit, then another day or so to emplace their mortars and check the range.

In bamboo thickets or heavy second-growth underbrush, infantry mobility was measured in tens of yards per hour as men took turns hacking through the greenery with machetes, sweating and cursing the thorns, vines, and hordes of clinging insects.

On the roads, troops could make 20 miles per hour in trucks, tanks, or armored personnel carriers. But one of the enormous antitank mines that peppered the roads of War Zone C could blow a vehicle into the air.

Helicopters could move troops at 90 knots—a great tactical tool, but requiring logistical agility. Troops might be slogging through heavy jungle growth, then receive an order over the radio for a combat assault. They would hack their way to a pickup zone, form into five- or six-man teams, and board helicopters. That meant flying a few minutes in the cool breezes at 1,200 feet, then swooping down into a hot, sweaty, and hazardous landing zone.

In early March, the high command began shifting major units out of the western part of War Zone C to engage enemy forces in its eastern part, closer to Saigon, but the 196th roamed through the area as a "floating brigade."

General Knowles recommended the floating brigade to General Westmoreland. "My main argument was that the usual process for collection of intelligence, staff estimates, briefings, and meetings

Artillery,
ammunition, and
C-rations are
dropped by
parachute to the
3d Bn., 82d
Artillery, the
196th's direct
support artillery
battalion, during
the first phase
of Operation
Junction City in
February 1967.
Throughout the
operation, the
196th, prized for
its ability to
quickly move
men and
machinery, was
deployed as a
"floating
brigade," able
to rapidly
engage an
enemy that
preferred to
make surprise
attacks and
then quickly
withdraw.

—so pertinent to conventional warfare—was just too time-consuming. The decision-making process and large-scale operations were robbing us of opportunities. We needed authority to act at the lowest practical level, and then to reinforce and exploit instantly any activity we could stir up. Almost all of the really good actions that we had started small. They were really meeting engagements, and we reinforced them as fast as we could. They were much like the old pile-on games we played when we were young."

With an economy of force, a single "floating" brigade kept the enemy off balance and inflicted continuous damage. From late March until 7 April, the 196th roamed through 600 square miles, operating day and night, and moving quick reaction forces on short notice to overwhelm enemy forces.

The long-term plan was to continue as a mobile brigade, however heavy enemy pressure far to the north changed that. Once again, the 196th had to show logistical agility.

Academy of war

Flying north to Task Force Oregon

AS 1967 BEGAN, evidence of NVA troop and artillery buildup within the demilitarized zone (DMZ) mounted. On March 20, heavy NVA barrages of artillery, rockets, and mortar fire hit Marine positions south of the DMZ. NVA troops crossed into Quang Tri province, ambushing vehicle convoys and attacking Marine outposts.

In early April, Westmoreland directed his chief of staff, Maj. Gen. Bill Rosson, to make plans for a task force of three brigades to head north to reinforce the Marines. The task force, to include the 196th Light Infantry Brigade, would be named Oregon, after Rosson's home state. The other two major units were 1st Brigade, 101st Airborne, and 3d Brigade, 4th Infantry Division.

However, NVA pressure on the Marines mounted so quickly that Westmoreland had to put the plan into effect right away. The 196th received first word by radio. The brigade's combat journal entry for 1127 hours on 7 April carried an alert order from the operations officer of 25th Infantry Division. Key staff officers from II Field Force Vietnam (II FFV) were en route to the brigade's base at Tay Ninh. They arrived in the afternoon with secret orders.

Knowles recalled: "General Weyand called me back to the 25th Infantry Division command post. He asked me how fast I could extract the 196th from our activities deep in War Zone C and then get them ready to move north—permanently. My response was to ask him how fast he could get the Air Force to bring C-130s into the airstrip at Tay Ninh. He asked what I meant. I told him that I would have troops and equipment ready to load on the C-130s as fast as they could land them, and I would continue

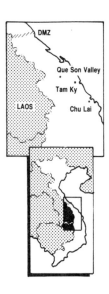

Academy of war

MOVING IN:
Stripped to the waist, men of the 196th string concertina wire along the outer edge of the perimeter of their new base camp at Chu Lai in April 1967. The move to Chu Lai to reinforce the Marines was part of a build-up to ward off an expected enemy offensive in the north of the country. One benefit of the move north was an escape from the southwest monsoon that was just beginning at Tay Ninh. At Chu Lai the northeast monsoon had just ended and the hot dry season was setting in.

that until we were totally redeployed. And that was what we did."

Two infantry battalions, the brigade forward headquarters, and supporting arms were far north of Tay Ninh, operating as the floating brigade. One battalion had just returned to base for area security. In short order the battalions in the field would disengage from the enemy, be helicoptered back to Tay Ninh, and prepare to fly north to Chu Lai. The first troop-carrying C-130 Hercules aircraft would

leave Tay Ninh in less than 36 hours, at 0600 on Sunday, 9 April.

The simple air movement plan was drafted overnight by the 196th staff and an Air Force airlift planning group. It was approved by midday on 8 April. Units would form themselves, vehicles, and equipment into modular C-130 loads and stand by in unit areas. The 7th Air Force would begin dispatching C-130s during the night of 8-9 April.

As C-130s flew into Tay Ninh airstrip day and

MOVING OUT:
A jeep is reversed onto the loading ramp of a C-130 transport at Tay Ninh in April 1967. The speed of the move north was a tribute to the 196th's "mobile state of mind." With an around-the-clock airlift the 196th switched base camps in less than a week.

night, they taxied into position on the ramp area. Waiting troops, vehicles, and equipment pallets flowed immediately into the aircraft. As a C-130 was loaded, its pilot was cleared for takeoff and flew north for Chu Lai, one and one-half hours away. The ramp had a capacity of four C-130s. However, by skillful maneuvering, the C-130 pilots crammed seven of their big birds into the space.

Daytime temperatures at Tay Ninh climbed to 100 degrees. Afternoon thunderstorms, harbingers of the southwest monsoon, cooled off the boiling ramp. The thin asphalt stuck to the C-130 landing gear, peeling off in strips. The airlift used 353 C-130 loads to fly 3,452 men, 973 vehicles, and cargo to a grand total of 8,285,000 pounds. The rear elements took up 33 more planeloads. The few vehicles and heavy engineer equipment that would not fit into C-130s drove to Saigon, were put aboard landing ships, and sailed north.

In less than a week from receiving the alert, the 196th Light Infantry Brigade pulled out of War Zone C, loaded up, and flew into a new base area. The western part of War Zone C reverted to the enemy.

A fringe benefit of the move to Chu Lai was the change in monsoon seasons. Around Tay Ninh the southwest monsoon with its torrential downpours was just beginning. At Chu Lai the northeast monsoon had just ended and the dry season was setting in. So the rot and fungus of the rainy season would be put off for months.

The northern part of Vietnam from Chu Lai back westward into the hills toward the Laotian border and northward to the DMZ would now be home to the 196th until the war's end. For now, however, the brigade's mission was to ensure the security of the Chu Lai base, its airfield, port, and other installations.

Maj.Gen. Bill Rosson —Commander of the three-brigade task force sent north to reinforce the Marines in April 1967. The 196th Light Infantry Brigade was one of the three brigades selected by Rosson. He named the task force after his home state— Oregon.

General Bill Rosson and his brigade commanders believed in an active defense, hunting the enemy. The Marines that left Chu Lai had been forced by events and their low strength into a passive defense close around the airfield.

The enemy forces were of three types. Local force VC were lightly armed part-timers who stayed near their villages. They set out booby traps, mined roads and trails, and acted as porters, scouts, and couriers.

Main-force VC were full-time fighters, well armed, trained, and equipped. They were organized and deployed in platoons, companies, and battalions with specific areas of responsibility. They had camps in the field.

The top rank was the North Vietnamese Army (NVA). Also well-armed and well-trained, they were kept in base areas in the mountains until ordered out by Hanoi.

Early in the life of Oregon, General Rosson attached two first-class combat units to the 196th: 1st Battalion, 14th Infantry ("Golden Dragons"), from 3d Brigade, 25th Infantry Division, and "Blackhorse," 2d Squadron, from the elite 11th Armored Cavalry regiment.

The 196th staff became accustomed to controlling many more units than its organic three combat infantry battalions. The number of battalions under 196th control could range up to six, seven, or more. For now, however, as the scorching 100-degree days of the dry season set in, the troops set out on their multiple missions.

Extracts from the brigade's combat log for Thursday, 27 April 1967, typify the wide variance of

actions on a "quiet" day. The combat log opened at 0001, and over the 24 hours, 77 entries were made.

In the early hours, the journal logged reports of patrols moving to ambush sites. Soon the routine ended.

0635: Delayed entry from 4/31. At 1900 the previous evening, the police chief of Binh Son reported that four men missing from the 4/31 were ambushed and captured on 21 April. The VC killed them that night, and buried them in the mud at grid coordinates BS626978. He also had information indicating a VC attack on 4/31 positions sometime between 26 and 29 April.

0640: D/4/31 sent a patrol to check the reported grave sites.

0755: 4/31 patrol departed to clear Hwy 1 in its area.

0817: Two-platoon patrol from Company B, 3/21 Inf departed base camp to conduct operations vic BS 5391.

0852: Company B, 3/21—Vietnamese child stepped on a mine or tripped a booby trap. Child taken to aid station. Dustoff helicopter requested for child.

0907: First lift of 1/14 Inf is airborne. (1/14 Infantry was conducting combat assault near the Tra Bong River.)

ACTIVE DEFENSE:
Men of the 196th search small boats on the Song An Tan River. Active defense meant hunting the enemy instead of waiting for him to attack.

Academy of war

BUNKER CHECK:
Pistol in one hand, survival knife in the other, a member of the 3d Bn, 21st Infantry, 196th Light Infantry Brigade, scans the darkened interior of a VC bunker before it is destroyed by an explosive charge. The bunker was typical of the type used by main-force VC, who established platoon-sized camps in the field away from the hamlets.

0926: Patrol from D Company, 4/31 found four fresh graves (near location reported by Binh Son police chief). Checking them out.

0930: First lift of 1/14 is complete; airlift of Battery B, 2/9 Artillery continues.

1010: 3/21 patrol is in contact at BS520908; received 30 rounds small arms fire from three spots. Searched area, negative results.

1026: Patrol from D/4/31 digging in graves found no bodies yet, but have found a 250-pound bomb. Requested explosive ordnance demolition team to blow it up.

1055: Company C, 4/31 airlift complete. Searching area.

1104: Delayed entry: at 0905, helicopter 912 spotted 100-150 Vietnamese moving south along a trail, carrying something on their backs. Group broke down into groups of three and four persons, continuing south. Airborne FAC will observe.

1105: Delayed entry: at 0001, US informer named Tra Ninh was assassinated in the village of Khuong Kho. Killed by a knife, assassin unknown. National Police investigating.

1120: 3/21 patrol received more small arms fire from estimated three VC. Returned fire, swept the area, VC fled northeast.

1308: Company C, 4/31 has 14 VC suspects; evacuating them for interrogation.

1310: C/4/31 requests Dustoff for one Vietnamese with a gunshot wound.

1315: Dustoff requested by 2/1 for small Vietnamese boy, 4-6 years old. Swelled arm, probably broken. LZ secure, will mark with smoke.

1430: 175th Engineer Company reports Seabees (naval construction personnel) working on culvert on Highway 1 received four rounds of small arms fire from west. Continued work.

1530: Company C, 4/31 Infantry found a tunnel at BT684048, shaft is 2×2×7 feet with two tunnels leading off at its bottom. Metal grate at bottom of shaft. Destroyed.

1630: Child that was evacuated in morning died of wounds at hospital.

1703: C/4/31 airlifted back to company base.

Heavy load —An ammo bearer takes a break after completing a patrol outside of base camp at Chu Lai in April 1967. The patrol along the east bank of the Tra Bong River in Quang Ngai province was one of hundreds conducted by the men of Task Force Oregon to keep the enemy off balance.

1816: 3/21 requests medevac for woman having a baby and hemorrhaging severely. Dustoff helicopter requested and sent. (Woman and baby flown to hospital.)

The remaining entries until midnight (2400) were routine on this day; patrols departing for night ambushes, situation reports from the units, night alert status.

With the addition of 2/11 Armored Cavalry and 1/14 Infantry, the 196th was strong enough to push far out into the countryside around Chu Lai, while preserving security of the base and the population thereabouts.

Task Force Oregon used its three brigades in an active role to control the populated areas of Quang Nam, Quang Tin, and Quang Ngai provinces. 1st Brigade, 101st Airborne, was committed around Tam Ky and westward into the hills, the former sanctuary of main-force VC and the 2d NVA Division.

Southward around Quang Ngai and Duc Pho, the 3d Brigade, 25th Infantry Division, pushed the local force and main-force VC enemy off balance. In the center, the 196th did the same.

Within two weeks after the 196th arrived at Chu Lai, General Rosson was selected for his third star, and Knowles for his second. General Westmoreland offered Knowles the command of Task Force Oregon, which Rosson would give up on promotion. Knowles accepted. His successor as commander of the 196th was Brig. Gen. Frank H. Linnell, who took over on 20 May.

Frank Linnell graduated from West Point in 1941. He led infantry units in combat in New Guinea and Luzon, ending World War II as a lieutenant colonel and battalion commander. He commanded a succession of infantry units from Korea to Santo Domingo.

Lt. Gen. Lew Walt, USMC, commanding III Marine Amphibious Force (MAF)—including Task Force Oregon—called Linnell to Da Nang. He said, "Frank, I don't care what the Army tells you to do— I'm telling you, don't let our airplanes and helicopters at Chu Lai be rocketed or sappered." Linnell recalled, "that was the clearest guidance I ever got. All the rest was vague: '. . . kind of surge

Academy of war

FORWARD AIR: USAF Maj. Bob H. Laurine, a forward air controller (FAC) working with the 196th, scans the ground for signs of enemy activity during June 1967 (top). The Plexiglass cockpit of his Cessna O-1 Birddog (bottom) serves as a scratch pad for noting messages and map coordinates. Maj. Laurine led the five fighter pilots serving as FACs with the 196th. With their radio call sign "Helix," they coordinated and delivered close air support. To men in contact with the enemy, there was nothing better than a call from Helix—it meant that fighter-bombers were on the way.

61

around and keep the Cong off balance. . .' and
'. . . win the hearts and minds.'" The Marine F-4s,
A-4s, A-6s, and helicopters remained unrocketed and
unsappered for many months.

For the soldiers and junior officers, the higher
strategies and command changes were somewhat
abstract. Their reality was the oppressive heat and
dust, constant sweat, and occasional fear. Mentally,
there was a need for constant vigilance, a state of
alertness, and a readiness for instant action. For the
tranquil countryside daily exploded into sudden
death.

Death came in many forms. On Highway 1 and
other roads within the area of operations (AO), land
mines were a major threat. Before traffic could run

each morning, the roads had to be cleared, a tough task requiring patience and skill. A section of road cleared yesterday could be mined today.

For roads out of unit sectors, mine-clearing fell to the engineers and cavalry: the 196th's own 175th Engineer Company and F Troop, 17th Cavalry; and the 2d Squadron, 11th Cavalry.

Magnetic mine detectors could not pick up plastic or wooden mines. Careful examination of the road-bed, shoulders, and ditches by experienced men would detect areas that had been dug and covered over. Then careful probing with pointed sticks or rods would reveal whether anything was there.

Or wires leading from a concealed mine might be found. They were for command-detonated mines,

HELIX DELIVERY:
Close air support summoned by an FAC: A USAF F-100 fires a rocket salvo into a VC jungle position.

63

where the VC would hide a few yards off the road waiting for a lucrative target, such as an ammunition or fuel vehicle.

When men encountered a suspected mine they proceeded very, very carefully. Kneeling in the dusty heat, they removed the dirt covering it. Once they uncovered it, they would either blow it in place with a demolition charge or call for explosive ordance experts to disarm it. If wires were found, the first action was to send an armed force down the wires. Most often the enemy would be long gone.

Land mines ranged from crude affairs made from TNT in a wooden box to Soviet or ChiCom crowd-killers of cast TNT weighing up to 50 pounds. US bombs that had not exploded were also used. With explosive charges of up to 200 pounds, those huge mines could—and often did—blow M48 tank turrets right off.

Booby traps were steady killers. They were often fashioned from ChiCom or Soviet hand grenades, operated by concealed trip wires. Worse yet, many of the booby traps were made from lost, abandoned, or stolen US hand grenades or 40mm grenade rounds. The VC rigged these wicked killers along footpaths or in bushes.

One particularly vicious patch for mines and booby traps was south of the Tra Bong River, in the the "Polar Bears" area. In 60 days, General Linnell noted that more than 60 men of Company A, 4/31, were killed or wounded by mines or booby traps. The grim saying was, "a foot a day in Company A."

Death also came from small arms fire, machine guns, rocket-propelled grenades (RPG), rockets, and mortars. That summer was a relentless series of small, sharp actions fought day and night. The land and seascapes were beautiful vistas, easily lulling the lazy or ignorant into mistakes. Days were hot and dusty, with midday temperatures reaching as high as 105 degrees. Men carried two, three, and four canteens of water, and topped them off at every stream or well.

The 196th also was required to work with Allied forces, which included the 2d ARVN (South Vietnamese Army) Division. US Air Liaison Officers of I Corps had reported that the ARVN 1st and 2d Divisions were content to control the coastal plains, following a "live and let live" policy with the NVA forces in the mountains to the west. When required, regular ARVN units would sally forth, requiring reinforcement by US manpower and firepower as a condition.

For example, 2d ARVN Division and the 196th conducted a large operation in August from Highway 1 at the Tra Bong River mouth some 18 miles inland through territory dominated by NVA and VC units. The objective was to cut through to the Special Forces/CIDG (Civilian Irregular Defense Group) camp at Tra Bong village back in the hills, kill enemy troops, and show that Allied power was being applied. A large convoy of ARVN and US trucks would drive into Tra Bong to reinforce the point.

The fair-weather dirt road to Tra Bong had been closed for ages. It was in enemy territory, heavily mined, and unused. To open it required a heavy mine-clearing effort and constant security against attack. But a leisurely and deliberate clearing would take weeks, giving the NVA/VC time to react in force. So heavy 2½-ton trucks were loaded with sand and backed up the road; infantry provided security. The convoy followed at a reasonable distance. When a truck encountered a land mine, it blew. If the mine was a small antipersonnel device, the truck kept

Cool as a mountain stream —Hot and exhausted, a PFC with a recon platoon takes a quick drink from a mountain stream in I Corp. The practice was against regulations. Men on patrol were issued water purifying tablets.

Academy of war

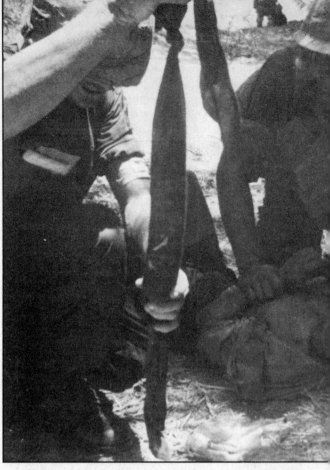

FACES OF WAR:
Two sergeants search a VC prisoner (left) and prepare to tie him with his own socks after his capture during Operation Hood River in August 1967. An infantryman (right) looks under a Vietnamese boy's sun hat for weapons during Hood River. Despite programs designed to bring the US forces and the indigenous Vietnamese closer together, the local population was always the subject of suspicion.

going. If it was a larger antitank mine, the truck usually was blown off the road. The brave drivers usually survived, shaken but unhurt. The disabled truck was pushed into the ditch and the next one reversed into its place.

During the night, tanks and armored personnel carriers of 2/11 Cavalry ran the cleared portion of the road continuously. Swiveling the tank searchlights and laying down searching fire from their machine guns, they prevented the enemy from remining the road.

The tactic worked, and the convoy reached Tra Bong. There, the true ARVN purpose became clear. Tra Bong was a center of cinnamon production. The annual crop, a large chunk of the world's supply, was ready to be trucked to market. Tons of rolled cinnamon bark were loaded into the trucks and rolled

back to Quang Ngai. Behind the cinnamon, the 196th and its units backed down the road, which soon reverted to its former closed state.

The brigade enjoyed tremendous support and cooperation from other US units. Its five Forward Air Controllers (FACs) and their men were led by Major Robert H. Laurine. The FACs were USAF fighter pilots detailed to Army units to coordinate and deliver close air support. Bob Laurine and his pilots lived with the brigade, flew day and night in support of its men, and were very much part of the family. Their radio call sign was HELIX, and they flew Cessna O-1 Birddog aircraft (later replaced by the O-2 Skymaster).

The brigade had its own organic aviation detachment, with UH-1 Huey utility and OH-23 observation helicopters. Its assets were augmented daily

Torching —A PFC in the 196th sets fire to a Viet Cong hootch during Hood River as part of a scorched earth policy that operated against enemy installations.

by direct support from 71st Aviation Company, "the Rattlers."

Another close bond was forged with Marine squadron VMFA-314, based at Chu Lai. VMFA's "Black Knights" F-4B Phantoms made a lot of noise screaming down the Chu Lai runway on full afterburner, but their big Phantoms with VW on the tail were quite welcome when they dropped bombs and napalm to help troops in contact.

Men had to learn quickly by experience. To ensure that they did not have to learn in blood, the Charger Academy was established. An intensive five-day indoctrination for all new officers and men, its faculty members were veterans who passed on hard-won knowledge.

The new men were particularly attentive after tripping booby traps. Instructors laid the traps on trails and other likely spots. When tripped, they popped with a loud black-powder charge.

At the Charger Academy, new men learned practical tips for survival: that sunglasses cut down their ability to spot trip wires; how the VC covered "spider holes" with bushes; how to distribute and carry the combat load without creating blisters or strained muscles; how to care for their delicate M-16 rifle; how to pick out a helicopter landing zone (LZ); and then, how to bring in choppers with colored smoke grenades and hand signals. The Charger Academy saved time and casualties in the line units, and made the new men productive, instead of liabilities.

After the academy, Thomas Grabowski, who had been in the Army less than five months, joined Company C, 2/1 Infantry as ammo bearer for an M-60 machine gun. "On my first day a squad leader in my platoon was killed. With only about 35 men in my platoon and 360 days left in the Nam, I figured mathematically I was looking at pretty bad odds."

He was 19 years old, with two years of college behind him. "Having watched different war movies over the years, I figured I would be nicknamed the "Kid." Only after getting into the field did I realize that everyone who was a grunt was either 18 or 19. I was one of the older ones."

Tom Grabowski and four thousand other men like him campaigned through the summer and into autumn of 1967. Heavy rains came early, deluging

the coastal plain with torrents of 15 to 20 inches in 24-hour periods. But when the rain stopped, searing sunlight blazed down again, turning mud into dust. Still, the three brigades of Task Force Oregon kept pressing the enemy. Contact was almost continuous in all three brigade areas in September and October.

In late September, Task Force Oregon was transformed into the 23d Infantry Division (Americal). Americal Division was formed in World War II in similar fashion from American regiments on New Caledonia, and fought alongside Marine units on Guadalcanal. The historical symmetry was apt. Maj. Gen. Samuel W. Koster arrived in October to assume command.

The Army gained another division in Vietnam without having to take one from its dwindling Stateside rolls. It also accelerated formation and deployment of two brigades destined for Vietnam (11th and 198th), and earmarked them for Americal.

Blood in the valley

Que Son Valley and the NVA offensive

ON 28 OCTOBER Americal Division issued the alert order: "198th relieve 196th at Chu Lai; 196th relieve 1st Brigade, 101st Airborne, northwest of Tam Ky." The 198th was to relieve the Chargers during 16–19 November, and 196th relief of 1/101 was to occur right after.

General Linnell was called south to become one of General Bruce Palmer's principal staff officers at Headquarters, USARV (US Army, Vietnam). Because the 196th was now part of the Americal Division with three generals, its commander's rank was cut back to colonel. Colonel Louis H. Gelling arrived from USARV to assume command. He was an armor officer, and combat-experienced.

In mid-November the relief was speeded up. Americal Division ordered the 196th to open its command post north of Tam Ky on 18 November, and relieve battalions of 1/101 rapidly over the next two days. The Chargers's command post and forward base opened for business at Hill 35.

By 21 November, 1/101 began flying out of Tam Ky south to Phan Rang. The 196th's friendly neighbor to the north was the superb 3d Brigade, 1st Air Cavalry. To the south, the new 198th was around Chu Lai. To the east was the sea, and to the west rose the high hills of the Annamite Chain. All around was the enemy.

The broad expanse of farmland and hills of the new AO was one of the most valuable between Chu Lai and Da Nang, strategically and economically. It had been fought over repeatedly since the Marines first ventured into it two years earlier. The Que Son Valley was contested by everyone, but belonged to no one. Its ground was soaked with the blood of Vietnamese and American men, shed in countless

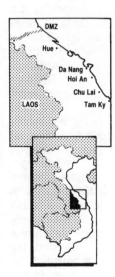

Blood in the valley

TREAD BREAK: Tank crewmen repair a wheel on an M-48 tank after removing the tread. The wheel was damaged when the tank hit a mine. Tanks from the 1st Squadron, 1st Cavalry, were assigned to the brigade during American Division operations. They were especially effective against enemy bunkers, first firing a high explosive (HE) round with delay fuze to kill the enemy inside, then a second, HE superquick, to open up the sides of the bunker.

small and large fights. The toughest and largest enemy force was the 2d NVA Division. With about 6,400 men, 2d NVA units emerged from the mountains around Hiep Duc at the apex of the valley to strike throughout the hills and lowlands of the region.

Fire support bases (FSBs) were established on three 1,500-foot hills overlooking the valley: FSB East, Center, and West. 4/31 Infantry was to establish FSB West; 3/21 Infantry on FSB Center; and 2/1 Infantry on East. Batteries of 105mm howitzers from 3/82 Artillery were assigned to each base.

The insignia of the Americal Division —Formed in the fall of 1967 and named after a famous WWII division that served in the Pacific theater, it numbered three brigades, including the 196th.

The northeast monsoon rains began early. Rain all morning on November 22 delayed airmobile operations. The helicopter lifts finally flew under a low overcast. Dim light filtered through the thick clouds, highlighting the dark greens of the jungled hills and the fields of the valley floor. It was a gray prelude to Thanksgiving Day.

At Gelling's briefing on Thanksgiving Eve, the brigade's logistics officer promised, "Every man will eat a hot turkey dinner tomorrow, no matter where he is." But events did not work out as planned.

An intelligence report was flashed to the 196th during the briefing. Units of the 3d NVA Regiment were reported to be entrenched near Hill 63, about 13 kilometers west of the brigade command post.

Task Force Dorland was nearest the enemy. Maj. Gilbert N. Dorland, operations officer of 4/31 Infantry who commanded the task force, had two 100-man rifle companies of the 4/31 Infantry. Two armor units were attached: most of F Troop, 17th Cavalry, in 15 of their M-113 armored personnel carriers, and a platoon of four M-48 tanks from 1st Squadron, 1st Cavalry.

Thanksgiving morning was overcast, with a 2,000-foot ceiling and misting light rain. Dorland's men gulped down cold C-rations, saddled up, and moved out westward in combat formation. One cavalry platoon rolled along with the troops. Its heavy .50-cal machine guns were welcome additions. The other tracks, about two miles to the east, began waddling across the soggy ground, spread out and alert.

Hill 63 rises like a pimpled island from the small fields of the flat valley floor. Its gently sloping sides are thick with hedge, underbrush, and jumbled

boulders. Houses, fields, and vegetable plots on the islands are separated by dense hedgerows and hedge fences. The ten-foot-tall hedgerows restricted visibility only to the next row, about 15 to 20 yards.

Colonel Gelling ordered 3/21 Infantry to put a rifle company on alert, and earmarked helicopters to stand by. Company B was designated and saddled up.

Just before 0700, Dorland's infantrymen worked their way slowly up the east side of Hill 63. Hunched over by heavy rucksacks, they walked in line formation, remaining in contact by radio. Captain Dan Mellon's Delta Company, 4/31 Infantry, found the enemy first. As they crossed the west face of Hill 63 at 0710, small arms and automatic weapons fire lashed them from the front, across the low paddies. Mellon's men flopped to the ground, shucking off their heavy rucksacks and returning the fire. Captain Jim Beierschmitt's Company B moved up on line, and also began receiving enemy fire. Both company commanders led their men forward, using all weapons to keep the enemy down. The deep *pum-pum-pum-pum* of the heavy .50-cal machine guns underlay the staccato chatter of the M-16s, the *rrrrrrrp-rrrp* of the enemy AK-47s, and the *crump-crump* of grenades.

The fight began at ranges of 20 to 50 yards. The distance narrowed as Dorland's men pressed forward, firing then flopping to cover others dashing ahead. NVA troops blazed away from camouflaged two-man foxholes until killed at close range.

Dorland's men needed reinforcement and resupply. Captain Dan Spahn's Company B, 3/21 Infantry, standing by for a combat assault on short notice, was loaded up in a dozen Hueys. Artillery concentrations and air strikes held the enemy down while the helicopters swooped in.

Captain Spahn's troops in the center were soon laying down heavy fire on the NVA. They fought well after landing in the hottest LZ any had seen. With their intervention, the neighboring companies could press ahead.

To keep the enemy from escaping to the west, Major Dorland called for supporting fire and reinforcements. 3/82 Artillery shifted six 105mm howitzers to the mission, dropping streams of 42-pound shells into the enemy 200 yards in front of the friendly troops. To cut off enemy escape southwest into the hills, the brigade called on Company C, 4/31 Infantry, led by Captain Joseph S. Stringham.

With B/3/21 and C/4/31 on the ground, and the arrival of the tank and cavalry platoons, the battle became a series of sharp, close-range fights against enemy bunkers in almost every hedgerow. The bunkers were dug into the hedgerow banks, with small firing apertures in front and escape holes in the rear. NVA troops waited until men were within 10 feet before opening fire. But the Chargers approached carefully. Once a bunker was located, the troops in front kept the enemy pinned down and maneuvered someone around the hedgerow to throw grenades into the rear exit.

Tanks and infantry worked together. The tankers used two rounds per bunker. First, a high explosive (HE) round with delay fuze to kill the enemy inside. The second, HE superquick, to open up the sides of the bunker. Against hootches or enemy in the open, the tankers fired canister rounds.

Air strikes and artillery hit on enemy positions farther back. By midmorning the area around and

Medal of Honor —Lt. James A. Taylor was with Troop B, 1st Cav, Americal Division, in November 1967 when one of his troop's armored assault cavalry vehicles was hit. He braved more fire to rescue five wounded, then rescued more men from a second burning vehicle. It exploded, wounding him, but he continued to engage the enemy—killing a three-man machine gun crew. He then rescued more men from a third burning vehicle before organizing a medical evacuation zone. For his valor he was awarded the Medal of Honor.

over Hill 63 was thick with aircraft and helicopters darting and swooping through the clouds and smoke of the battle. The overcast lifted to about 5,000 feet, giving the brigade's FACs more room to bring in the fighter-bombers. A slight breeze started blowing. It mixed the colored smoke used for signaling with the white, gray, and black clouds from explosions and fires.

Dustoff medevac helicopters flew in low to avoid the F-4 Phantoms and Huey gunships. Seven men were killed and nearly 50 wounded in the first two hours. Maj. Gil Dorland was one of the severely wounded. But Lt. Col. Jack Thomas, the 4/31 battalion commander, had arrived and took over. The

Dustoff birds whipped in through the streams of tracers and clouds of smoke to fly the wounded to the brigade clearing station at Hill 35. The nine-mile flight took five minutes. Resupply helicopters with ammo added to the aerial traffic congestion.

One position defied all grenades and small arms fire for an hour. Finally, an enterprising platoon sergeant prepared an improvised satchel charge. He tied eight pounds of TNT on a 12-foot bamboo roof pole, twisting electric wire from the blasting cap on the TNT along the pole to his detonator. His men kept up heavy fire on the bunker's apertures while he prepared the charge and wriggled into position. On his signal, their fire slackened. The NVA troops

THE THIN GREEN LINE:
Co C of the 2/1st Infantry working through marshes along the bank of the Song An Tan River while searching for VC activity in October 1967.

Forward hole —A forward artillery observer uses a ready-made foxhole for cover as he communicates with his battery via a PRC-25 radio during the course of a search-and-destroy operation by Co C, 3d Bn, 21st Infantry, 196th Light Inf Bde. Forward artillery observers frequently joined frontline patrols to help locate the enemy and call in fire support.

popped up and began blazing away through the front apertures. The sergeant stuck the satchel charge in the rear entrance, slid back into the hedge, and detonated the charge. The blast caved in the bunker and killed its occupants.

By nightfall on Thanksgiving Day, 60 enemy dead had been found in captured positions. The Americans had suffered seven men killed and nearly 50 wounded. The enemy was still fighting from strong bunkers, and seemed to have plenty of ammunition. The 4/31 Infantry and attached units dug into a tight defensive perimeter for the night.

Before dark, 3/21 Infantry under Lt. Col. Allen Champlin was alerted to make assault by helicopter at first light into an LZ about 1,000 yards northwest of the fight. Champlin's men would block enemy movement or reinforcement and work toward 4/31 Infantry to clear the area.

During the night of November 23-24, Air Force flareships stayed over the battlefield. Artillery flares popped under the high overcast, bathing the battlefield in a ghostly silver light. As the flares descended, their shadows lengthened and darkened. It was an eerie yet noisy scene. Small enemy groups probed the perimeter.

RTO (radio-telephone operator) Richard Carey with his PRC-25 radio was curled up in a foxhole near his company commander. "That night it seemed all the artillery in the world crashed down in front of us. I remember moving out to the front the next day. Jesus to Jones, there was a spider hole not 15 yards from where we had been."

The day after Thanksgiving dawned overcast and humid. Lt. Col. Champlin's 3/21 Infantry helilifted to block escape to the northwest. Thomas's 4/31 Infantry resumed their slow, methodical clearing of the islands, working with tanks and cavalry. Artillery and air strikes continued in support. At mid-afternoon, a 20-man NVA platoon broke out to the northwest. They were all killed.

The pattern continued that day and the next. Thirty more men were wounded; all survived, thanks to the skill and prompt actions of the platoon and company medics and quick helicopter evacuation.

On the morning of the 25th, Company D, 4/31 Infantry, swept slowly across one small bushy island

Blood in the valley

FIRE SUPPORT:
Men of A Battery, 2d Bn, 11th Artillery, fire an M114A1 155mm howitzer in support of Americal Division units, operating in the Duc Pho area in November 1967. Whenever possible infantry patrols remained within the nine-mile range of the 155mm howitzers for immediate fire support.

Blood in
the valley

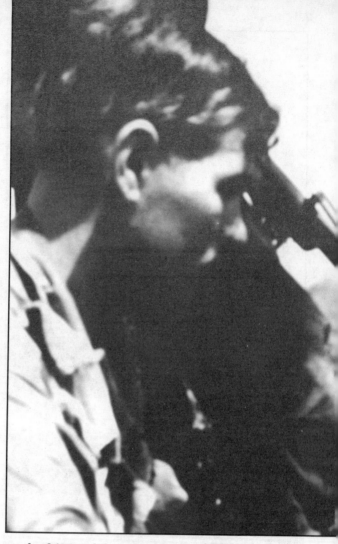

EXPLOSIVE HEDGEROW: A fire team leader prepares a TNT charge to blow up a hedgerow for fear that it could be of use to the Viet Cong during a search-and-destroy operation near Chu Lai in October 1967. Enterprising infantrymen would often resort to the use of TNT in improvised satchel charges when conventional means of destroying enemy positions either failed or were unavailable.

on the fringe of the area. From experience in other battles, they turned about and swept back again very deliberately, probing into the foliage with rods and sticks, flushing out several more enemy soldiers. After probing the patch twice, Captain Dan Mellon ordered one more sweep. Three more NVA soldiers were found and killed.

On the battlefield were found 56 weapons, much equipment, and 151 enemy dead. Documents identified them as from the 5th and 7th Companies, 3d NVA Regiment. The weapons were new and in good shape. That afternoon, Thanksgiving dinner was

finally flown in to the men of Task Force Dorland.

An intriguing footnote was that several men reported seeing a six-foot-two Caucasian "round-eye" on the other side. From then until the following May, occasional similar reports came in after contacts with the 3d NVA Regiment.

After the battle, companies of the 196th spread out from the three main firebases and the brigade base to flush out the NVA in the Que Son region.

At each base was a battalion combat command post, one rifle company, an artillery battery, and the usual mix of engineers, signalmen, medics, and

Blood in the valley

SIGNAL CITY: A forest of VHF signal masts marks a typical infantry base camp in I Corps in 1967. Each base camp consisted of a battalion combat command post, one rifle company, an artillery battery, and a mix of engineers, signalmen, medics, and other specialists.

other specialties. The other rifle companies of each battalion humped the hills and streams for 10 to 14 days at a time. They were resupplied by helicopter every fourth or fifth day. When contact was made, artillery and air strikes were turned on, helicopter gunships appeared, and reinforcing companies flew in immediately.

The trick was to find the enemy before he found you. That meant days and nights on end being wet and cold. (Nighttime temperatures in the hills in December and January dropped to the high 40s, frigid indeed for men accustomed to the 90s.) It meant moving stealthily and concealing your presence, so you ambushed the enemy, not the other way around.

Find the enemy —before he finds you was the grunt's motto. An infantryman takes a break during operations. His pack, weighing up to 60 pounds, was a burden that no grunt ever fully accepted.

Tom Grabowski recalled a day when Company C, 2/1 Infantry, was moving carefully in the backwoods. "I was walking point down a little river. I guessed it seemed safest from booby traps. I was in water about chest high, when the bottom suddenly dropped off. My rifle and helmet were never seen again." He was burdened down by 50-60 pounds of gear, and sank fast. "Luckily, I was able to bob over to the bank without taking in too much water. The bobbing technique was something I learned in the physical education class at the University of Delaware."

Grabowski dried off as he moved. Before long, his company flushed an NVA unit. "We had the NVA on the run and the gunships were giving us support. One of the door gunners mistook me for the enemy— I had borrowed a cap, since my helmet was gone. The only thing that saved me was that the copilot turned around and pushed the door gunner's machine gun out of his hands."

The 196th began a pattern of continuous combat patrols. Battalions were assigned large areas, and subdivided areas for their rifle companies. Within its area, each company commander decided on patrol routes and methods. The result was no discernible pattern, but complete coverage of the area, preventing the enemy from establishing strong positions or massing forces. Patrols always remained within the seven-mile range of the 105mm howitzers of 3/82 Artillery for immediate support.

In early December an intelligence windfall was reaped deep in the Que Son Valley by B Troop, 1/9 Cavalry, a first-rate aerial reconnaissance unit.

Insignia of the "Blues" —B Troop of the 1st Sqdn, 9th Cav. Serving as a reconnaissance squadron of the 1st Cavalry Division (Airmobile), it possessed three troops. The Blues was the division's internal designation for an aero-rifle troop, red was for aero-weapons, and white for aero-scout.

Enemy ground fire hit the commander's gunship. He marked the spot, kept it under observation, and lifted in his experienced rifle platoon (the "Blues"). The Blues, supported by gunships firing rockets and machine guns, landed to take the ridge where the enemy troops were emplaced. In a fierce fight, they wiped out the tenacious NVA soldiers. A search of the bodies turned up a bonanza.

Matt Brennan, one of the Blues, described the scene in his book, *Brennan's War*. "Souvenirs were everywhere on the knoll. We grabbed pistols, compasses, Chinese binoculars, map cases, pouches of documents, and rifles. One of the maps had the crossed sabers of the 9th Cav still visible under the plastic. It had American positions marked in red and Communist positions marked in blue. It was the same system we used—good guys in blue and bad guys in red." (1985, Presidio Press.)

On that hilltop had been the command section of the 3d NVA Regiment, accompanied by senior officers from 2d NVA Division staff. Of the 17 men the Blues killed, nine were officers, including one full colonel and the political commissar of the division.

Markings and symbols on their maps and overlays pinpointed positions of the 196th and its neighboring 3d Brigade, 1st Air Cavalry. The hill where the NVA officers died overlooked one of 3/1 Air Cav's firebases, LZ Ross. Included in the plan were approach routes, assembly areas, and attack positions, just as if they had been drawn at Fort Benning.

The symbology forecast a heavy assault on the firebases, and soon. The senior NVA officers were clearly on a personal preattack reconnaissance. According to solid intelligence, headquarters of 2d NVA Division had moved forward and was now at the mouth of the Que Son Valley.

When would the attack come? The Christmas truce was three weeks away. After it? Or after the New Year's truce, a week later? Or would the NVA change their plans? They could not fail to know that the plans were probably compromised.

It was decided that the brigades in Que Son should prepare as if the enemy would attack as planned. Given past behavior, he would probably break one of the truces or attack immediately afterward.

All units were briefed to expect the NVA attack at year-end. Observation of the area intensified, but the low overcast and rain interfered. The overcast hung at 2,000 feet above sea level, only a few hundred feet above the firebases.

LZ Ross belonged to 3d Brigade, 1st Air Cav. It was FSB West's nearest neighbor deep in the valley. Captain Charles Krohn, the intelligence officer of 2d Bn, 12th Cavalry at Ross, analyzed past NVA/VC attacks on firebases. The pattern: heavy mortar and rocket fire was poured on the objective to put the Americans' heads down. While the GIs hunkered in bunkers, enemy sappers blew through the wire, then fanned out. Assault troops followed. Krohn's orders were succinct: when the mortars come, keep your head up, watch, and catch the sappers in the wire.

Christmas and its truce came and went with occasional sniping. Intelligence reports began to indicate that the regiments of 2d NVA Division were moving into position as planned. The New Year's truce passed quietly. Then all hell broke out in the Que Son Valley.

A few minutes after midnight on 2–3 January, the 3d NVA Regiment poured hundreds of rounds of

FIREBASE SUPPLY:

Men of Battery A, 1st Bn, 82d Arty, Americal Division, unload 155mm howitzer rounds from a five-ton truck at a heavily defended firebase. Wherever possible the firebases were positioned on high ground to command approach routes and shared overlapping fields of fire with neighboring firebases.

mortar and rocket fire onto LZ Ross and LZ Leslie (also of 3d Brigade, 1st Air Cav). The flashes and *crumps* of the explosions could be heard for miles and flickered on the low clouds like fiendish northern lights.

At 0348, mortar rounds began dropping on FSB West. Within the hour, Company D, 4/31, on ambush out in the valley NW of West, reported 60 to 70 NVA between them and the firebase. They began shooting at the NVA, who went to ground. If this was the offensive, then it was time to consolidate the patrolling companies. Single companies were not strong

enough to overpower NVA battalions in the open. Units of 3/21 and 4/31 Infantry linked into task forces of two companies each, under command of the senior captain.

Thus began a week of continuous unrelenting combat between regiments of the 2d NVA Division and two US brigades. Neither rain nor darkness saw the fighting abate. It only died down when units on either side broke contact, then surged again after they were reinforced or resupplied. At LZ Ross, Captain Krohn's analysis and orders paid off. When the heavy mortar barrage came, the troops of 1/12

ENEMY HQ:

An innocent-seeming hut in the Que Son Valley. It was used as a base by the 2d NVA regiment for surprise attacks during January 1968.

Blood in the valley

QUESTION TIME:
A Viet Cong suspect in traditional black pajamas is questioned by a member of the Popular Forces, the Vietnamese militia that worked closely with US troops. Battlefield interrogations frequently yielded useful information about the enemy's intentions and the impact of US actions.

Cav kept their heads up. They were ready for the sappers and assault troops, killing 242 in one night against the loss of one.

At the firebases, the thin security forces held against occasional sappers reinforced with mortars, rockets, and even French 75mm artillery shells. The bloodiest battles raged in the tiny hamlets, paddies, and streambeds at the mouth of the valley. At first, the two-company task forces held their own. Then enemy reinforcements and heavy fighting hurt them hard. The 196th reinforced 4/31 Infantry with companies of 2/1 and 3/21 Infantry, creating heavier task forces.

Dry language in the combat journals cannot evoke the reality of the close fighting in the mud and rain. But the journals and recollections after the battle begin to tell the story. Here are typical extracts from the 196th Brigade combat journal, night of 5-6 January:

1800: C/2/1 CO and platoon leader wounded, dusted off. The senior lieutenant took command.
1935: C/2/1 in heavy contact again. (10 minutes later: C/2/1 request help ASAP!!)

Artillery and helicopter gunships were directed

to help the beleaguered company.
2025: 71st Avn ("Rattlers") gunship shot down north of C/2/1.
2036: C/2/1 surrounded and receiving fire from all sides.
2040: C/2/1 has NVA inside its perimeter.
0044: A/4/31 linked with C/2/1.

From 2050 until 2245, Charlie Company remained in heavy contact. They were hit with small arms, automatic weapons (including 12.7mm machine guns), and mortars from all directions. They fought back hard, taking casualties but killing the NVA attackers. At 2245 they were holding on, and receiving only a few hand grenades. Apparently the enemy was regrouping.

The nearest friendly force was about 1,200 yards away: Company A, 4/31 Infantry, under Captain Larry Byers.

Insignia of the 4th Bn, 31st Infantry —known as the "Polar Bears." They served as part of the 196th Light Inf Bde, being officially transferred to the Americal Division in February 1969.

Captain Byers recalled: "We could see the muzzle flashes from the enemy (attacking C/2/1). I received orders at 2050 to move Company A to reinforce. We requested 81mm illumination to help us see our way off Hill 445, because there was no moon. Traveling was slow." By 2340, his company had overpowered several enemy automatic weapons positions and was within 400 yards of Charlie Company. But the enemy attack on Charlie Company resumed.

Byers's outfit was guided toward Charlie Company by radio contact with its artillery FO (forward observer), 1st Lt. Bromley H. German. Lieutenant Drake, the acting CO, was fighting to save Charlie Company. Lieutenant German was directing artillery and mortar fire on the NVA, as well as rallying the beleaguered infantrymen and talking Captain Byers into position to link up.

Byers went on: "By 2400 hours, the acting CO had been killed." Lieutenant German took charge. Byers's company got within 75 yards of Charlie Company. "Lieutenant German was killed at that time, and only the RTO was left on the radio. He and I organized signals by which my elements could be recognized as they entered the perimeter. By 0010, 6 January, my point man made contact with Charlie Company."

Byers's company found Charlie Company almost dissolved from the heavy fighting. Twelve of its men and three others (including Lieutenant German) were dead; 43 were wounded. Eight men were still okay. The company had repulsed continuous assaults, including three "human wave" attacks by six enemy rifle companies.

The battle continued for the rest of the night. Byers's company beat off repeated NVA attacks, sustaining 12 wounded. Medevac helicopters could not come in because of the continuous fighting. Overcast and low ceiling prevented close air support,

Blood in the valley

ENEMY DEMO: Dressed in the black pajamas and sun helmet of an NVA soldier, a US soldier demonstrates how a Chicom rocket-propelled grenade launcher was used on the battlefield.

but at first light helicopter gunships from the Rattlers arrived. Their rockets and machine guns supplemented Byers's fire, pushing the enemy away from his perimeter.

Meanwhile, 4/31 Infantry had dispatched its Companies C and D toward the fight. By 0745, the enemy broke contact, moving north into the hills. Dustoff helicopters flew in, flying out 54 wounded men to the brigade clearing station and onward to hospitals; 186 enemy dead strewed the field.

Frequent enemy contact continued throughout the Que Son Valley, as the 2d NVA Division pressed its offensive. No one had to encourage the men to wear

their armored flak jackets and steel helmets, or to keep their weapons ready. Close air support missions by USAF, Navy, and Marine fighter-bombers were scheduled daily. But the heavy monsoon weather scrubbed half of them.

During Sunday night, NVA gunners were busy. At 2125 they fired 122mm rockets and assorted calibers of mortars onto LZs Ross and Leslie. By 2305 the air base at Da Nang was under rocket attack. At 0200 Monday morning they blasted Charger Hill, the 196th command post, with 82mm mortars.

On Monday, the fighting intensified. Company D,

Operation Medcap —A doctor serving with the 4th Bn, 31st Inf, examines a Vietnamese child during a Medcap operation, a civilian aid program designed to increase rapport between the US troops and the civilian population. Thousands of patients were treated for everything from imagined illness to pneumonia and tuberculosis.

3/21 Infantry, and Company B, 4/31 Infantry, made up Task Force Oscar. D/3/21, commanded by Captain Roland Belcher, was searching from east to west into the area where Charlie Company, 2/1 Infantry, was hurt badly two nights before. B/4/31 moved in parallel a few hundred yards to its north. At noon each company set up a perimeter, put out security, and began a C-ration meal. A helicopter bringing in ammunition to Belcher's company reported NVA troops nearby. Belcher sent out three 10-man patrols, saddled up the rest of the company, and started to follow. They spotted troops crossing a field and gave chase. Soon the company came under intense automatic weapons and mortar fire and became split. Belcher with his command group and part of one platoon were separated.

Once again, Captain Byers and his stalwarts of Company A, 4/31, were near the hottest fighting. He commanded Task Force Herman—his company and Company A, 3/21 Infantry. Captain Joe Stringham commanded Task Force Lise, also nearby. It was his own company (C/4/31) and B/2/1. Both task forces started toward the sound of the fighting around Belcher's unit. A heavy rain was falling and the overcast settled on the hilltops. Medevac, command, and resupply helicopters were forced ever closer to the ground, becoming fat targets for the NVA 12.7mm machine guns. Belcher's separated company began to take heavy casualties from the superior enemy force dug into a horseshoe ambush.

Byers's task force pressed through the rain. His lead platoon spotted 75 NVA troops heading toward Belcher's beleagured unit. Byers called for artillery support, but so many missions were being fired that 30 minutes passed. By then the enemy was adding to the hordes assaulting Belcher's separated forces. By mid-afternoon, 1448 hours, the last transmission was heard from any of Belcher's radios.

Near sunset the enemy units began breaking contact, leaving their dead and a few wounded on the field. Survivors of Belcher's company withdrew into the relative safety of Byers's task force. NVA automatic weapon and mortar fire continued to fall as friendly units organized night defensive positions on totally inadequate terrain. They could not move west into the hills because the NVA were there, nor to the east without being exposed on the move.

Byers set up a perimeter, including 58 survivors from Belcher's company. Twilight came early; scattered clouds hung at 300 feet, and the overcast descended to 1,000 feet. The NVA stayed close.

Disposed into a tight two-company defensive perimeter nearby, Captain Joe Stringham recalled: "There was so damn much enemy activity around our location during the night. The tracers and blasts from the repeated rifle firing gave the appearance of Times Square on New Year's Eve. The torrential monsoon storm poured unusually hard during the night. By 0300 we were all standing in our foxholes waist-deep in water."

Contact continued for two more days, waning then surging again as the NVA units pulled back westward toward the mountains. Resupply helicopters had to fly low under the overcast, meat for enemy 12.7mm machine guns.

By the morning of Thursday, 11 January, the NVA offensive in the Que Son Valley was over. The brigade had lost 64 men killed. The enemy left 429 bodies on the battlefield, and hundreds more in the area of 3d Brigade, 1st Air Cavalry next door. Troops of all units had fought well in the muck and blood of the dark green valley.

ENEMY FIREPOWER:
A Chicom 122mm rocket launcher displayed by the 196th as part of a weapons haul. The most powerful portable weapon in the enemy inventory, it was effective over six miles.

Miracle of arms

Stamping out fires

THE TET OFFENSIVE started early on Tuesday, 30 January.

In the Que Son Valley and along Highway 1, the situation was quiet at the end of January and early February. The action was happening around provincial and district capitals. Main-force VC units tried to take Tam Ky, capital of Quang Tin province, but ARVN defenders rose to the occasion, helped mightily by the continuous presence of helicopter gunships and C-130 "Spectre" gunships. Using the easily seen Highway 1 as a coordination line, the gunships hosed down the waves of attackers, killing more than 600 and enabling ARVN troops to hold on.

Farther north, Da Nang and Hoi An were hard hit with rocket attacks followed by ground assaults. NVA and VC units captured Hue, Vietnam's third-largest city and former imperial capital.

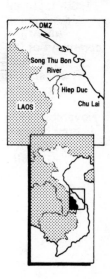

Da Nang now became a focal point for the 196th, which now had six strong battalions to deploy. Its own three plus 1/6 Infantry and 2/35 Infantry and the 1/1 Cavalry were all dependable fighting units. The resolute 1/1 Cavalry operated north-south along the axis of Highway 1, from the seacoast to well inland. It kept the highway open, interfered mightily with VC movement in the coastal region, and worked with the 5th ARVN Regiment (stiffening its resolve and activity). An air cavalry troop, C/7/17 Cav (the "Blue Ghosts") was attached, to add its mobility and reconnaissance skills.

Troops of the 1st Regiment of the 2d NVA Division were taking control of the ground immediately south of the air base's parallel north-south runways and threatening the huge Marine-Army helicopter base at Marble Mountain. Marine troops were hard-

Insignia of the 1st Bn, 6th Inf —Known as "The Regulars," and with an authorized strength of 920 men, they served with the 196th Light Inf Bde, coming under the command of the American Division in February 1969. Then in November 1971 they became part of the 196th.

pressed to hold Da Nang. Americal was ordered to help out. Koster turned to the 196th for two tasks. First, reinforce 3d Brigade, 4th Infantry Division, with one battalion to help in the fighting around Hoi An. (2/35 Infantry had already been released to its parent 3/4 Brigade.) Second, Colonel Gelling was ordered to take a task force north—ASAP—to relieve the pressure south of the Da Nang air base. He created Task Force Miracle, composed of 2/1 and 1/6 Infantry, plus supporting arms. Within hours it was heading for action.

On 8 February Task Force Miracle passed to operational control of III MAF and deployed to the sandy lowlands immediately south of Da Nang air base. In four days of fighting they wiped out the threat to the base.

The fighting was so close to Da Nang air base that USAF and Marine fighter-bombers took off to the north, gained altitude, rolled back southward, and dropped their bombs, all in less than five minutes.

1/6 Infantry was nicknamed "The Regulars." Lt. Col. William J. Baxley's men epitomized the nickname during the battle at Lo Giang. Intense fighting began soon after they landed in a hot LZ on 8 February. Close hand-to-hand fighting developed against tenacious and dug-in NVA troops. Company G, 2/3 Marines, was attached to Baxley's battalion. The Army-Marine battalion closed against the 60th Battalion, killing 266 enemy while losing 15 men. The deaths in 1/6 Infantry were relatively low because Baxley insisted that his men wear flak jackets and steel helmets at all times. Of the 55 men wounded, 43 percent were in the legs or torso below the waist; another 39 percent were arms or neck, areas unprotected by flak jackets or steel helmets. Of the protected areas (torso, waist up, and head), only 17 percent were hit.

For its extraordinary determination at Lo Giang, 1/6 Infantry was awarded the Army's Valorous Unit Citation. Its men created the "miracle" that Task Force (TF) Miracle was sent to Da Nang to accomplish. TF Miracle was dissolved on 13 February, and brigade headquarters returned to its forward base at Charger Hill (Hill 35). Its AO expanded north and west, covering the area formerly the responsibility of two brigades.

Units of the 196th ranged for two months over the

Miracle of arms

PROTECTIVE COMMANDER: Lt. Col. William J. Baxley (right) commander of 1st Bn, 6th Infantry, otherwise known as "The Regulars." Combat fatalities in 1/6 Infantry were relatively low because Baxley insisted that his men wear flak jackets and steel helmets at all times.

Miracle of arms

larger area of operations. Heavy contacts occurred occasionally, as in early March. The usual pattern was days of relentless patrolling interrupted by sharp firefights, explosions of mines or booby traps, or the *whooooosh* and *crump* of incoming mortar rounds at night. For the moment the gray, wet days of stand-up battles against NVA battalions were past. Also, the northeast monsoon was abating, and the prospect of dry days was ahead.

The infantry battalions formed reconnaissance platoons (recon) to expand their scope of patrolling. Brigade had its own LRRP, the long-range reconnaissance patrols, which were inserted far back into

the mountains to watch trails, detect enemy base areas, and act as long-range eyes and ears. Recon platoons operated closer in. Stealth and jungle skills were the best insurance for survival, together with the men's closeness to each other. Operating in small groups, the men were in peril if discovered by the enemy.

At Khe Sanh, Hue, and generally across the two most northern provinces, hard fighting continued. By mid-April the siege of Khe Sanh was over. After the diminution of enemy threats in the south, Westmoreland moved the 101st Airborne and 1st Cavalry divisions into the Hue/Phu Bai area. Now that Hue

Insignia of the 2d Bn, lst Inf —One of the original battalions that comprised the 196th when it was formed at Fort Devens and one of the first to arrive at Tay Ninh in August 1966. From February 1969 until November 1971, it—along with other 196th battalions—was part of the American Division. From December 1971 until its departure from Vietnam seven months later, it was again part of the 196th.

was retaken and Khe Sanh relieved, it was time to reenter the A Shau Valley.

For more than two years, the NVA had built up a strong base area in the valley, 32 miles southwest of Hue. In Operation Delaware, Westmoreland ordered the 1st Air Cav to head south from Khe Sanh toward the A Shau. The 101st Airborne with an ARVN regiment would push westward into it from Hue/Phu Bai. Air mobility was the key to overcoming the 4,000-foot mountains protecting the A Shau on the east, and was the key to keeping the troops on the move in the enemy base area.

On 17 April, the 196th was ordered to Camp Evans, 15 miles northwest of Hue. The mission: Under operational control of 1st Air Cav, to become the reserve brigade for the provisional corps. Gelling's units saddled up in a fashion long familiar to the 196th: Take essential weapons and combat equipment, leave nonessentials behind, and move out.

During its month-long stay in Operation Delaware, the 196th was not committed as a brigade. However, its 3/21 Infantry was detached on 1 May and sent to help out the 3d Marine Division around Dong Ha, flying into blocking positions with the Cua Viet River at their backs. The "Gimlets" fought alongside the Marines for more than two weeks.

On 6 May, 2/1 Infantry, commanded by Lt. Col. Robert B. (Buck) Nelson, was released to operational control of 101st Airborne. Buck Nelson's 2/1 Infantry was in good shape, and was accustomed to rapid movement and quick engagement. The men had faith in each other, essential for combat survival.

Nelson's original mission was to protect a major bridge and secure the 101st's north flank from the sea to near the mountains. He put his battalion command post in bunkers at the bridge, and fanned his companies by helicopter. Using what he called the "grasshopper" technique, reconnaissance helicopters with an artillery FO aboard would comb the area. "When they received fire, I inserted the reserve company. It was not unusual for us to have three air assaults in a single day. The 2/1 kept the area quiet and piled up a good tally (of NVA/VC) with minimum losses."

Nelson also followed a basic combat precept that was hammered into every unit of the 196th: know

Staff Sgt. Nicky D. Bacon

MEDAL OF HONOR

Staff Sgt. Nicky D. Bacon was serving with Co B, 4/21 Infantry, at Tam Ky in August 1968 when it came under fire from an enemy bunker. When first one and then another platoon leader fell wounded, S/Sgt. Bacon assumed command and led successful assaults against the bunker and an enemy machine gun position, killing four VC. In an ensuing action he climbed on the exposed deck of a tank and fired on an enemy position while his men rescued the trapped and wounded. For his gallantry he was awarded the Medal of Honor.

exactly where every one of your units is located, and report the locations accurately.

Troopers of 2/1 Infantry grasshoppered around for several days, keeping the Hue area quiet. On 10 May three companies of 2/1 Infantry were in contact with enemy forces at three different points, none serious. Colonel Gelling arrived about midday with orders. Nelson was to disengage, assemble his battalion at Hue/Phu Bai, and fly into the Special Forces/CIDG camp at Kham Duc to relieve the garrison. Kham Duc was under heavy NVA attack, and needed help fast.

One by one the 2/1 companies broke contact, made their way to helicopter pickup zones, and were lifted to Hue/Phu Bai airfield. There they transferred quickly to USAF C-130 transports. The flight to Kham Duc only took 30 to 40 minutes, but it was a jarring transition into a different world. From the sandy coastal plains, the 2/1 troopers shifted to a battered black asphalt airstrip flanked by red dirt and surrounded by dark green mountains towering

WASHING THE DOG: An instructor shows a dog handler with the 196th how to keep his dog from overheating when on a patrol.

two to four thousand feet above its 1,115-foot elevation.

At Hue/Phu Bai, Buck Nelson landed for a briefing and onward transport. "I was handed a set of maps with the Special Forces camp circled, told to relieve them, and ushered onto the C-130. It did not take me long to determine they knew little more about the situation than I."

Battery A of 3/82 Artillery was the normal direct support for 2/1 Infantry. Its six 105mm howitzers were emplaced at Kham Duc to fire on targets out to 11,000 yards. The 4.2-inch mortars of Nelson's battalion were positioned to provide close-in coverage, supplemented by the 81mm mortars of his three rifle companies. Every round would be needed,

because Kham Duc was more than 50 miles beyond any friendly supporting artillery.

Tom Grabowski was in Nelson's Company C, with eight months of combat behind him. "When we were brought in to guard the perimeter it seemed like a cake job, since we had been out in the field for months on end." That impression was soon erased. Kham Duc was besieged by an estimated 5,000 to 7,000 NVA troops.

Nelson was the senior man on the spot and was charged with the mission of relieving the camp. He soon discovered his radios could not link with those of the Special Forces and Delta teams. Nor did he have radios capable of reaching American Division headquarters, 60 miles over the mountains. He could

Gen. William C. Westmoreland —US commander in Vietnam. He had to decide whether the Kham Duc special forces camp should be held. He decided it should not.

talk to the forward air controllers overhead, but they could not relay back to Chu Lai.

Nelson disposed his companies around the western, northern, and eastern ground, covering the best approach route. Special Forces and Delta teams closed the south part of the ring, where a river gave some protection from surprise attack. Outside the perimeter were three outposts manned by CIDG irregulars. To each outpost, Nelson sent a reconnaissance team with a forward observer to adjust artillery and mortar fire. He also got a radio that was supposed to reach Chu Lai, although contact was sporadic because of the weather and the distance.

Troopers of 2/1 Infantry and A/3/82 Artillery did not need urging to dig. They were experts at digging. It meant survival. Nelson said, "By next morning (Saturday, 11 May) we were completely dug in and mostly covered.

That morning, NVA diversionary assaults came from the south, across the Dak Se River, to be repelled by the Special Forces and Delta camps. The main attacks came from the north, when a company-sized unit charged down the gentle slope. Company A drove back the attackers. One of the 105mm howitzers took a direct mortar hit; the gun crew were killed or wounded and the howitzer destroyed. The rest of the day was quiet, except for frequent incoming mortar rounds.

General Westmoreland had to decide whether Kham Duc should be reinforced further and held, as Khe Sanh had been. He ordered Maj. Gen. Sam Koster at Americal to abandon the camp. Koster flew to Kham Duc to pass the word to Buck Nelson.

Over the night of 11–12 May the NVA probed the essential outposts and the Special Forces and Delta camps. The outposts were overrun and lost by daylight. Tom Grabowski recalled the scene: "We knew things weren't going well when we woke up and the outposts had flags other than American."

During the night Nelson requested close-in B-52 strikes to break up the attackers. Only one was delivered, along the river. At dawn, Company A repelled another major attack and Company B took probes. Now the evacuation began. An Air Force combat control team (CCT) was on hand to help control C-130s and C-123s flying in to evacuate the

MEDAL OF HONOR

Platoon Sgt. Finnis D. McCleery

Platoon Sgt. Finnis D. McCleery was serving with 1/6 Infantry in May 1968 when his men were pinned down by enemy fire during an assault on Hill 352, 17 miles west of Tam Ky. With extraordinary courage P/Sgt. McCleery made a one-man assault on the enemy bunkers. As the 40-year-old Texan ran across 60 meters of open ground, bullets and grenades exploded at his feet. He began firing from the hip and throwing grenades and, even though, by now painfully wounded, he continued to advance and penetrated enemy lines. Wounded again, he then signalled to his men to assault Hill 352 while single-handedly he continued to destroy enemy positions. For his heroism he was awarded the Medal of Honor.

1,000 men of the Special Forces/CIDG garrison and 2/1 Infantry. FACs flying overhead controlled an increasingly heavy flow of fighter-bombers.

After the outposts were lost, NVA antiaircraft guns were established on the ridge lines at both ends of the runway, with heavier concentrations on the southwest ridge. Nelson asked for napalm to be dropped on the positions to reduce the risk to the C-130s coming in. "Very little was dropped," because the fighters carried mostly high explosive bombs.

"With the heavy air traffic we soon ran out of white phosphorous and smoke rounds to screen the approach and departure routes. We passed a message through the FAC for aircraft to avoid the ridge southwest of the runway. Taking off in that direction, aircraft were to make a sharp left turn to the south as soon as their wheels were up. "This was done by all aircraft except one loaded with Vietnamese. The plane flew directly over the ridge and

Miracle of arms

HEROISM AT KHAM DUC: This photo (left), taken during the rescue of three men isolated at Kham Duc Special Forces camp on 12 May 1968, is believed to be the only photo taken during a combat action in which the Medal of Honor was won. The C-123 piloted by Lt. Col. Joe M. Jackson is on the center of the runway at the top half of the picture. At the right edge are the three survivors running toward the C-123. Moments after the photo was taken a 122mm rocket was fired at the C-123. For his heroism in rescuing the three, Lt. Col. Jackson (right) was awarded the Medal of Honor.

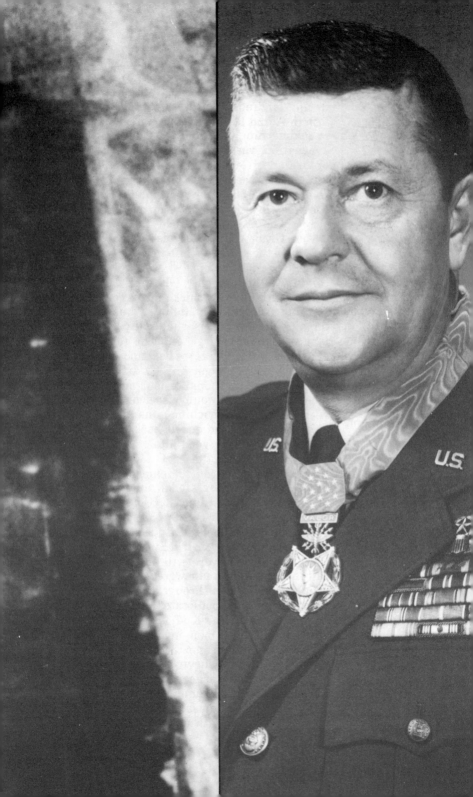

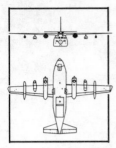

The C-123 Provider —Tail number 542 of the series was flown by Lt. Col. Joe M. Jackson during the rescue mission at Kham Duc. One advantage of the 75-foot-long C-123 was its ability to put down and take off from only 1,800 feet of runway. At Kham Duc, Jackson had barely 2,200 feet.

was immediately blown out of the air. There were no survivors."

Nelson deployed Company C to lay down suppressive fire along the north edge of the runway during landings and takeoffs.

Both A and B companies repelled major assaults in midmorning, helped by air strikes. By noon the evacuation was moving along so Nelson gave the order to destroy everything possible. Only Nelson and part of the reserve platoon from Company C remained at 1500 hours. They made a quick tour of the now-tiny perimeter, then piled into the last C-130. The afternoon rainstorms were closing in.

Tom Grabowski, who was in the last platoon, described the scene. "While we were waiting for our plane (the last one out) we could hear the enemy coming. I thought only GIs were that loud. The brush was extremely thick and we could hear them hacking away. Finally, fighter planes arrived with napalm. I think that is what really held them back long enough for us to get out. The napalm was close enough so we could feel the heat and smell the bodies burning. Once we got on board the plane, after leaving all of our supplies, our only thought was whether the plane would rise above the mountains with the 12.7mm machine guns taking direct aim at us. The plane did get us back to Da Nang, but it took some pretty good hits."

Three men missed the last C-130 out of Kham Duc. The USAF combat control team (CCT) were still in a hole when the aircraft left and fighter-bombers began blasting the camp. Lt. Col. Joe M. Jackson, who was piloting a C-123, No. 542, in a holding pattern at a 9,000-foot altitude south of the camp, heard an animated voice over the radio warning that three US airmen were still on the ground. Radio calls to CCT went unanswered. The C-123 ahead of Joe Jackson landed through heavy fire to pick up the men, but could not locate them. The pilot poured on the power and lifted off. Just as he did, the crew spotted the three men in a ditch bordering the runway—too late to stop. Joe Jackson was next. In the ditch, the CCT survivors figured they had two choices: be taken prisoner or fight to the end. With 11 magazines of M-16 ammo left, they chose to fight. T/Sgt Mort Freedman said, "We were going to take as many of them with us as we could." However,

Miracle of arms

MAIL CALL:
Mail is unloaded at an Americal Division supply depot at Chu Lai in May 1968. High command recognized the importance to morale of letters from home and through an elaborate supply network made sure that even the men at the front received regular mail. Regular re-supply to patrols in the jungle every fifth day included a hot meal, clean clothes, C-rations, ammo, and mail.

111

Col. Frederick (Fritz) Kroesen —took over command of the 196th in May 1968. His one-year tenure was the longest of any 196th commander in combat.

Joe Jackson fooled the AAA (antiaircraft artillery) gunners. Flying his lumbering C-123 like a fighter, he dove toward the strip, pulled up a quarter-mile from the end of the runway, and set up a landing attitude. A burning helicopter blocked the runway, leaving only 2,200 feet. Burning ammunition exploded around the area. Jackson set his C-123 down at the runway end and stood on the brakes, stopping just short of the burning helicopter. The three CCT survivors scrambled aboard over the rear ramp. While Jackson turned the aircraft around, a 122mm rocket slammed into the ground 25 feet in front. Jackson and his copilot waited in horror for it to explode. It did not. Joe Jackson taxied around the rocket and jammed the throttles to the firewall.

"We hadn't been out of that spot ten seconds when mortars started dropping directly on it. That was a real thriller. I figured they just got zeroed in on us, and the time of flight of the mortar shells was about ten seconds longer than we sat there taking the men aboard." As the aircraft picked up ground speed and swerved around craters, tracers arced at them in a cross fire.

Miraculously, the cross fire did not stop No. 542, and the aircraft lifted off the ground, slowly picking up speed and climbing out of the valley. For his extraordinary heroism and profound concern for his fellow men, Joe Jackson was awarded the Medal of Honor.

The companies of 2/1 Infantry were soon reassembled and deployed to FSB Baldy, where the 196th had just returned from Camp Evans. Within a week 2/1 Infantry was fully manned and reequipped. It soon flew out west to LZ Ross and resumed regular patrolling in the western Que Son Valley and mountains to the west.

Tom Grabowski recalled the daily routine in a rifle company. Four or five companies would patrol out from a base camp (such as FSB West, or Buck, LZ Ross or Baldy). One company secured the firebase.

Whether on the firebase or patrolling, he said, "every night was guard duty. That meant no one slept more than three hours a night for months on end." If your company was patrolling, you got up before sunrise and humped two or three miles away from your night position before eating a C-ration breakfast. Then you patrolled through the morning.

ADDING TO THE FAMILY

WHEN the 196th became part of Task Force Oregon in April 1967, additional battalions were attached to it and operated with it for long and short periods. This soon became standard procedure. As additional units were attached, the brigade's staff and its support battalion simply added them to the family and got on with the business of fighting.

This list from a combat after-action report gives some idea of the inherent flexibility of the 196th, showing how many units were attached to it in a year of fighting between 11 November 1967 and 11 November 1968.

1/1 Cavalry	1/52 Infantry	Vietnamese forces:
4/3 Infantry	C Troop, 7/17 Cavalry	5th ARVN Regiment
1/6 Infantry	10th Combat Tracker	6th ARVN Regiment
1/20 Infantry	Team	RF and PF Forces
4/21 Infantry	51st Infantry LRRP	CIDG Forces
2/35 Infantry	Teams	MIKE Forces
1/46 Infantry		

"We would break for lunch, which always meant more C-rations, then continue patrolling. Usually in late afternoon we would find our night position. Sometimes we would eat before getting into our night position; other times we would wait.

"Every fifth day we were resupplied. This meant one hot meal, clean clothes, mail call, and a new batch of C-rations and ammo." The C-rations were heavy and bulky. "Most of us preferred to go a little hungry rather than carry five days of food along with everything else we had to carry. Even though the days seemed boring, this was the type you prayed for in going through the 'big countdown' (to rotation)."

At the end of May, command of the 196th changed. Lou Gelling had been in the job nearly seven months, longer than the norm at that time. He had continued the high standards of leadership and the positive and flexible attitude throughout the brigade's ranks. Gelling's successor was Colonel Frederick J. (Fritz) Kroesen. An infantry platoon leader and company commander in World War II, Kroesen commanded a battalion of the 187th Airborne Regimental Combat Team in the Korean War as a major. Westmoreland, his regimental commander, remembered Kroesen's extraordinary achievement of making a night withdrawal during a ChiCom offensive on sudden notice in the middle of "a black and sodden night"—probably the most difficult of infantry maneuvers.

Harvest of death

Far out west and trouble-shooting

COLONEL KROESEN commanded the 196th longest in combat. His tenure (May 1968 to May 1969) also spanned a period of profound change.

Lyndon Johnson announced in March 1968 that he would not be a candidate for reelection. Martin Luther King was assassinated in April. On 12 May Kham Duc was evacuated and peace talks began in Paris. Robert F. Kennedy was killed in June. Massive protests disrupted the Democratic Convention at Chicago in August. Richard M. Nixon was elected president in November. His Secretary of Defense, Melvin R. Laird, announced "Vietnamization" of the war in March 1969. In April, US troop strength in Vietnam peaked at 543,400. In May, President Nixon proposed a peace plan for Vietnam including mutual troop withdrawals.

Meanwhile, Colonel Kroesen and the 196th continued to excel. Battalions new in Vietnam, such as 4/21 Infantry, were sent out to them for seasoning. Others, such as 1/52 Infantry, were placed under the 196th's wing when it got them out of trouble.

The 196th faced many tests in the second half of 1968: from fighting the old foes of 2d NVA Division to ensuring the rice would be harvested; from night ambushes to resettling refugees; and from 105-degree heat to 50-degree cold.

Colonel Kroesen saw his mission as denying a huge area to the tough and skilled enemy. Each battalion kept three companies in the field patrolling, and one on the firebase. Kroesen charged each battalion commander with entering and searching every grid square (1,000 × 1,000 meters) in areas of about 20 kilometers square. "The men understood that they were safer, more secure, by staying on patrol and keeping the enemy off balance." This

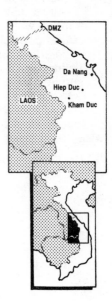

Milk delivery —Men of the Reconnaissance Platoon, Co E, 3d Bn, 21st Inf, 196th Light Inf Bde, enjoy cartons of chilled milk dropped while out on patrol. Efficient helicopter resupply meant that patrols could spend several weeks away from base.

constant humping took energy and determination, but it was far safer than sitting in a hole waiting for an enemy attack.

Americal Division intended to preempt enemy attacks by pushing troops farther west into the mountains than ever before. Task Force Cooksey was formed under command of Brig. Gen. Howard Cooksey, one of Americal's assistant division commanders. The operation was called Pocahontas Forest.

To provide Cooksey with the strength needed, the 196th thinned troop strength in its AO and released three battalions: the experienced 4/31 Infantry and the relatively new 4/21 and 4/3 Infantries. On 7 July they attacked west across the Song Thu Bon River west of Hiep Duc.

TF Cooksey's force leapfrogged westward, establishing firebases to keep its maneuvering battalions within 105mm artillery range. For a month Cooksey's battalions violated the formerly sacrosanct area in the mountains around the Song Thu Bon River and its tributaries such as the Song Tranh. This was true "Indian country," the stronghold of NVA units for years. Friendly forces had penetrated only as long-range reconnaissance patrols.

When TF Cooksey was dissolved after a month the 196th was ordered to redeploy to retain some of the far western territory under friendly control. Additional battalions were attached. In August, brigade strength was seven infantry battalions plus 1/1 Cavalry. (An infantry division had nine battalions.) Kroesen thinned out strength along the coast and in the main Que Son Valley to free up maneuver units to control the western territory.

The area under control of the 196th between August and September 1968 measured more than 800 square miles, which meant reliance on helicopters for resupply and long periods of carrying heavy loads in the jungled hills.

The jungle could be friend or foe, depending on your outlook. In fact, it was neutral. Arthur Askeland of 3/21 Infantry reflected on his feelings. "As a young green 20-year-old soldier, the thought of going into the jungle (let alone to fight an unseen enemy) was frightening. Like the name of our Recon platoon, 'Spectre,' the jungle represented a deadly fear. The first time in the jungle where I could sit back and look at it was beautiful and enchanting. It was so green, fresh, and alive with foliage and vegetation that I had never seen before. The jungle offered refuge from the scorching hot sun, yet misery in its wet, humid denseness when patrolling. For our small recon platoon, the jungle gave us life, as we could be concealed from the enemy.

"Yet in its quietness, death stared at us because of its isolation from help. In an enemy jungle, life and death can be measured in seconds. Something few people can understand unless you were there. But the jungle was also an exciting, thrilling, and breathtaking time—if you survived."

While pushing at NVA units in the far west, the 196th continued to be responsible for security of the population in the Que Son Valley and along the coastal plain. They worked closely with ARVN units in the AO, and the RF/PFs (Regional/Popular Forces) in the hamlets. This took patience and tact, as well as alertness.

By mid-September American Division brought in the units hung way out to the west. The northeast monsoon would prevent helicopter operations in the mountains.

Also, with the rice harvest about to start, heavier troop strengths in the populated farming areas were needed. The firebases out west were dismantled and the distant units moved back eastward around Hiep Duc and the old firebases.

Life on a firebase was a respite from humping heavy loads through the jungles. It was a chance to receive mail and hot chow, to write letters, to ease the strain just a little. But the flip side was perimeter guard duty at night and living in bunkers. Art Askeland recalled one. "I was in charge of one bunker with two new troops on FSB East (Hill 488). The first night we had a rat problem. Cat-size rats jumped on our chests or scurried by our heads as we slept. Outside the bunker, the VC tried to crawl close to the position and throw grenades. Luckily they had to throw uphill and could not get close enough to be effective. We beefed up our position with more trip flares, claymore mines, and sandbags. We also got a box of rat poison from supply.

"Next night in the bunker we heard the rats yell and squeal as if they were dying in great pain. One of the new guys said, 'That rat poison is really

Friend or foe —An infantryman crawls on his belly through the jungle to return VC sniper fire with his M-79 grenade launcher. To young soldiers, the jungle was both friend and foe—a retreat from the hot sun and a natural habitat for the enemy.

Harvest of death

SNIPER!
The still of an
Americal
Division
firebase is
suddenly
disturbed as an
enemy sniper
opens fire and
infantrymen
dive for cover
(right) as they
try to scan a
nearby woodline
to locate the
enemy position.
The incident
took place north
of Quang Ngai
City in April
1969. For men
who had been
humping
through the
jungle, a week
at a firebase
was considered
a rest—until
incidents like
this.

Harvest of death

MEMORIES:
A "Donut
Dolly's"
scrapbook
memories of
pleasant times
at Charger
Hotel, the rest
and recreation
center created
at the 196th's
base at Chu Lai.
Safe inside the
perimeter,
weapons
handed in for
checking and
maintenance,
men relaxed,
slept, and
stopped facing
death for three
days. The
young woman is
"Larry" Young
from North
Carolina. She
was one of the
American Red
Cross "Donut
Dollies" at the
Americal. They
took recreation
programs to
units in the
field.

working.' That night and the next we slept with no
rat problems.

"The fourth night we worried about VC sappers
sneaking up to the bunker and throwing in a satchel
charge, blowing us up. As it was getting dark, the
three of us were standing behind the bunker talking
and looking over our position. We heard a loud
thump on an air mattress, as if someone had thrown
something through the front window. As I reached
down to grab my M-16 leaning against the bunker
door, a large common cobra was coming out. I
jumped back! One new guy dropped his food tray and

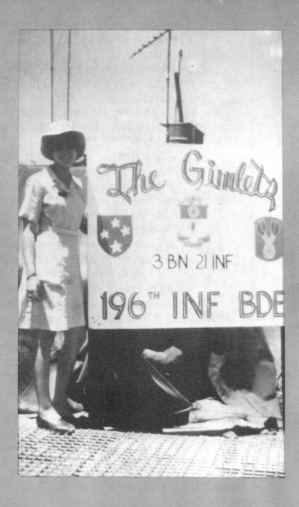

ran; the other new guy picked up a shovel to defend himself. As the snake came out of the bunker, he zipped around the corner and headed in the right direction—down the hill toward the VC!"

An even better treat for the rifle companies was a stay at the "Charger Hotel" at brigade rear on the Chu Lai base. Colonel Gelling had established it when the brigade moved away from Chu Lai in November 1967, and Colonel Kroesen put it to regular use.

CH-47 helicopters would fly a company out of its battalion firebase to Chu Lai every six to eight weeks. It was a time for them to clean up and sleep, party some, and for three days be free of facing death.

Every autumn a major problem was the rice harvest. The NVA and VC needed the rice; so did the local citizens and refugees. There was never enough in a country that once exported rice. Even with its population depleted, the Que Son Valley was a major rice bowl. Buck Nelson's 2/1 Infantry mounted "Grim Reaper" to bring in the rice.

Nelson said, "At dawn each day the village chief, RF/PF commander, and I would fly over the area at grasstop. By midmorning they had selected the rice fields that were ready. That afternoon I inserted a rifle company with attached RF/PF platoon to secure the area and set up an outer perimeter. At dawn the next morning, I inserted the RF/PF company.

"When all was secure, the big CH-47 helicopters would bring in the harvesters: men, women, and children. It was a riot watching them load into the CH-47s and fly off. They were unloaded in the field they were to harvest. Cargo nets were spotted around the area for them to deposit the harvested rice. When the nets were full, the CH-47s picked them up and flew them to the village soccer field. Immediately the old men, women, and younger children beat the rice from the stalks, piled the stalks for straw, and moved the grain to storage. We continued this for almost four months, harvesting

RUFF PUFF CONSULTATION: A lieutenant in the 196th consults with members of the local Vietnamese militia—the Regional Force/Popular Forces, nicknamed the Ruff Puffs—about an operation in the Que Son Valley. Cooperation between US and local forces was vital in bringing in the rice harvest, which otherwise would become a source of revenue and supply to the enemy.

about 1.5 million pounds of rice. The entire operation was run with very few casualties. Those we had came from booby traps."

Bringing in the rice harvest kept the NVA and VC units in the valley off balance. Hard fighting was another method. Michael J. Crescenz, a 19-year-old corporal in A/4/31 Infantry, gave his life in one short, sharp fight near Hiep Duc. Company A had run into a large and entrenched NVA unit on a patrol. The initial burst of NVA gunfire from two bunkers killed the two point men and pinned down the lead squad, holding up the entire company. Without hesitating, Michael Crescenz seized an M-60 machine gun and charged 100 yards up the slope. His blazing bursts of fire silenced the positions and killed their occupants. He charged a third bunker, killing its two crewmen and putting it out of action.

Company A started moving again when suddenly intense machine gun fire erupted from another camouflaged bunker. Although heavy enemy fire was directed at Corporal Crescenz, he assaulted the position with his machine gun. He was within five meters of the enemy gun when a final burst killed him. His heroic and selfless actions enabled Company A to maneuver freely and complete its mission. The Medal of Honor was awarded posthumously for his extraordinary heroism at the cost of his own life.

By January 1969 the western areas were considered safe enough to return several thousand refugees to their homes. Most had fled from Hiep Duc and hamlets around it in 1965. This was a high point for the American operations in the Song Thu Bon Valley. It was evidence that aggressive patrolling could hold an area and deny it to the NVA/VC, an example not lost on the 2d ARVN Division and the province and district chiefs.

The situation along Highway 1 and the coast was also reasonably quiet, with only light contacts. The 5th ARVN Regiment had come to the 196th AO, and plans were made to operate together. Outside the villages and in the hills, however, NVA and VC units were preparing to strike Tien Phuoc, a prosperous village on the Song Khang River, and capital of its district. A no fire zone (NFZ) encompassed Tien Phuoc and the neighboring village of Hoi Lam.

A Special Forces/CIDG camp with a short airstrip and heliport was there, across the river from the

Medal of Honor —PFC Michael J. Crescenz, awarded the Medal of Honor posthumously for his gallantry in overrunning three enemy bunkers in the Hiep Duc Valley in November 1968. Without regard to his own safety, he continued to ignore intense enemy machine gun fire and stormed a fourth bunker. As he came within five meters of it, he was hit by enemy fire and was mortally wounded.

Medal of Honor —SP4 Thomas J. McMahon, a medical aid man awarded the Medal of Honor posthumously for his bravery in rescuing two men wounded caught in enemy fire. Despite being wounded himself, McMahon dashed back to rescue a third man, when he was cut down by enemy fire.

main settlement. Established in November 1965, it was operated by Detachment A-102. A hard-surface dirt road led from Tien Phuoc eastward through the hills and flats to the province capital at Tam Ky, 16 miles away.

In May 1967 the 3d Bn, 5th Marines bloodied—and were bloodied by—the 21st NVA Regiment on the hillsides north of Tien Phuoc. Now in March 1969, the 3d NVA Regiment infiltrated troops to cut off Tien Phuoc. Americal Division sent 1st Bn, 52d Infantry, to attack from the southeast. In eight days of fighting from bunker to bunker, 1/52 Infantry was ground down and unable to continue.

Americal finally took action that was days overdue. It attached 1/52 to the 196th, extended brigade boundaries southward to include the battle area, and gave the battle to Kroesen. He committed three battalions. Lt. Col. John Brandenburg's 3/21 Infantry flew in first, and took charge. It pressed hard against the 3d NVA; 2/1 and 1/46 Infantries added their weight two days later. 1/46 Infantry crossed the Song Khang River west of Tien Phuoc to block NVA escape. Men of 2/1 Infantry, supported by engineer demolitionists and flamethrowers, joined 3/21 Infantry in reducing the 3d NVA positions one at a time. It was hard going, a series of intense firefights at 10 yards range.

Specialist Fourth Class Thomas J. McMahon, a medical aid man with Company A, 2/1 Infantry, earned the Medal of Honor. Lead elements of Company A were taking heavy enemy fire from fortifications close at hand. Three men fell, seriously wounded. Tom McMahon dashed from cover, ignoring his own safety, to the wounded men. He administered first aid to one man, then pulled him to safety. He dashed through the fire to aid a second man. A mortar round exploded at his side while he was dragging the man in, wounding McMahon himself. He refused medical aid and dashed painfully back for the third man. Heavy enemy fire cut him down and, mortally wounded, he died before reaching the man he was trying to save.

About the time the 196th was fighting at Tien Phuoc, Secretary of Defense Melvin Laird announced "Vietnamization" of the war. To President Nixon and Secretary Laird, Vietnamization meant turning over the war to Vietnamese armed forces

Harvest of death

RIVER CROSSING: Men of the 196th on patrol north of Chu Lai use a combination of rope and air mattresses to keep their equipment dry as they cross a river. The lattice of waterways in the region meant that a patrol could get thoroughly wet several times over in the course of a day. Skin disease caused by prolonged exposure to wetness was a constant problem and standard operating procedure was to dry out after each crossing.

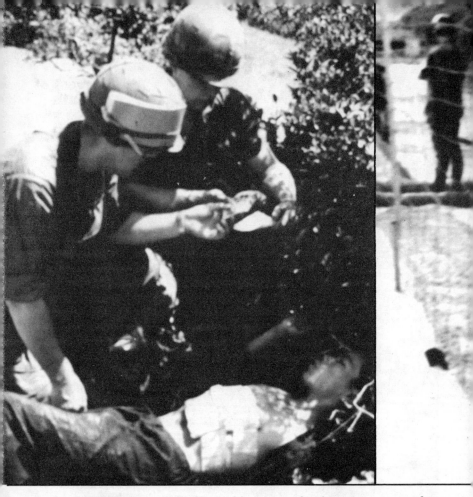

gradually and bringing the American troops home in phases. It defused protests at home, but made no real difference on the battlefield. ARVN troops were not ready to take over the war, at least not in the Americal area. The NVA and VC units continued to sally forth on order to demonstrate that. The next major fight was at the province capital of Tam Ky. Once again 3/21 Infantry was called for the heavy work.

Capt. Ernie L. Carrier commanded Company C, 3/21 Infantry, during the 1969 fighting. He had served as a platoon leader in another brigade, earning the Silver Star for gallantry. After that, he served on the Americal Division staff. He extended his tour in Vietnam to command a rifle company in 3/21 Infantry.

"I was lucky in that I got assigned to a company with some combat veterans that knew their enemy and the area well. My expectations were met in every way. The men were a hodge-podge, with every ethnic and religious background available. I knew right from the start some were on drugs and some were alkies. I told all of them that if I ever found one of them stoned in any manner that the next firefight would be their last because I would put a bullet in them. All of us were responsible for each other, and I would do my utmost to keep them alive and I expected the same of them." Carrier and his men got along fine.

Carrier's company operated like the enemy, at night. "We would work an area for three weeks and take notes on the terrain, people, dogs, hootches,

ABOVE: A detainee raking sand at the POW Collection Point. Prisoners could only be employed at labor required for normal camp maintenance.

Medal of Honor
—PFC Daniel J.
Shea, a medical
aid man
who was
posthumously
awarded the
Medal of Honor
for his gallantry
in braving
enemy fire to
rescue four
wounded men
near Tam Ky in
May 1969. When
he returned to
rescue a fifth he
was cut down
by enemy fire.

where fresh gardening was, trails (lightly or heavily traveled), anything of interest. The week we were on FSB Center, we would go over and over these notes in small groups and as a company. When we left the hill we would operate only at night."

Carrier and his men carried heavy loads, particularly ammunition. He was resupplied only once a week: "No sense letting him know where we were. Basic load was 36 M-16 magazines, and some guys carried more. M-79s carried 72 rounds of HE (high explosive), and shotguns 10. 1,200 rounds per M-60 machine gun. Six M-26 fragmentation grenades per man. We cut the handles off our toothbrushes to make room for ammo. I wanted some staying power, since we had eased up on about 800 NVA one night carrying rockets on poles. That was plumb scary, with only 89 men. We let them pass on by and called artillery on their route."

Meantime, Kroesen's year in command of the 196th ended. He was succeeded by Col. Thomas H. Tackaberry.

The 1st VC Regiment of 2d NVA Division overran a regional force (RF/PF) outpost near Tam Ky on 12 May, threatening Tam Ky. 1/1 Cav was committed against the hilltop outpost, but needed help to take it. 3/21 Infantry was committed, flying Companies B and C into the battle.

Carrier recalled, "I didn't like the operation from the start since we were getting dropped in the afternoon (little daylight left) and my lift had 13 birds. (I was still superstitious then.) I also knew that we were going into something big."

His men were concerned about the door gunners. They had heard that if the enemy shot at the flight going in, the gunners were pushing people off the craft a little early and high up. "I told the flight leader about it, and told him that my people had been given orders to drag the gunner off with them if pushed, and we would let him be a grunt for a few days. I ended up with two new people that day. My guys took me to heart and when pushed, they pulled."

The LZ was in a dry paddy with woodlines on both sides. Carrier's helicopter was shot down, but everyone got out. His company moved out with two platoons in front. The point man saw NVA troops stringing communication wire. Carrier pulled back

a few yards, began firing his mortars, and called in air strikes. His men heard NVA gunners firing 12.7mm AA machine guns at the aircraft, *thump-thump-thump*. Presence of the 51s meant an enemy regiment was there. His company held all night in their perimeter, suffering only mortar fire and no ground attacks.

Next day was bright, dry, and hot. Orders came to move out to retake the RF/PF post. They had an open area of about 125 yards to cross. Several men from the lead platoon were wounded in the first hail of fire and lay sprawled on the hot dirt. PFC Daniel J. Shea, 22, from Norwalk, Connecticut, one of the company medics, saw the men fall. Shea dashed forward into the intense fire, to help the wounded. He made four trips to pull wounded men into the perimeter. Shea spotted a fifth man lying in front of one of the enemy positions. He ran forward again, but was hit and grievously wounded. Dan Shea disregarded his wounds and sprawled next to the other man. He tended the man and began dragging him back toward the perimeter. Before he could

MINE CUTTER: A former VC demonstrates how enemy sappers under cover of darkness cut the wires to disable claymore mines around US perimeters. Once perimeter security was lost, defending troops were at their most vulnerable.

Harvest of death

DUSTOFF:
An Americal Division team prepares to load a wounded Vietnamese child aboard a Medevac helicopter, call sign "Dustoff," at Landing Zone Buff. Although LZs were made as secure as possible, they were frequently targeted by the VC as points of vulnerability— the risk being highest when a helicopter came in to land.

reach it, a heavy burst of fire killed him. He was awarded the Medal of Honor posthumously.

Captain Carrier: "(The rice paddy) wasn't much, but the berm provided some protection from the withering fire. NVA gunners were firing into the position from three sides. Panic was the order of that hour. The troops dropped their rucks as they pulled back. In them were most of the ammo, including machine gun and grenades. A helicopter tried to bring in fresh ammo, but was driven off by the heavy enemy fire. "We dug a foxhole with helmets, since

the entrenching tools were on the rucks that littered the rice paddy.

"The night was hell. I started the day with 89 men and ended up with 37. We used close air support all that night. The jets dropped nape close enough to burn the perimeter. When I ordered the hard stuff along the same lines they refused. Hell, we were in hand-to-hand combat, catching grenades and throwing them back. Nine sorties of 'Spooky' (AC-47 gunships) saved our butts."

During the all-night battle, NVA troops fired RPG

and 57mm recoilless rifle rounds into the perimeter. Artillery illuminating flares helped hold them back, but when the flares burned out the NVA crept closer. Carrier and his leaders redistributed ammo all night, and his men kept the NVA at bay.

However, Company B, ARVN companies, and 1/1 Cav were pressing the NVA regiment. By sunrise, they prevailed. The outpost was retaken and the 1st VC Regiment withdrew. Outside Carrier's tight company perimeter lay 34 NVA bodies.

For the first two weeks in June, 3/21 Infantry distinguished itself again against NVA units threatening Tien Phuoc. For sustained distinguished heroism as a unit from 13 May to 17 June, the 3/21

Infantry (with A/2/1 attached) was awarded the Army's Valorous Unit Citation.

In August, 3/21 and 4/31 Infantries (along with 5th ARVN Regiment) took heavy casualties in battles against NVA forces northeast and south of Hiep Duc. The resettled refugees were prospering in Hiep Duc, and this rankled the NVA. The enemy high command moved units toward Hiep Duc from the west. In a coordinated operation, 7th Marine Regiment pressed southward from near Hoi An and 4/31 Infantry moved to the northeast from Hiep Duc. Both American forces ran into heavy resistance from strong entrenched NVA units at every ridge line. Instead of pinching off the nascent NVA offensive,

the troops found themselves slogging one bunker at a time in heat that often reached 120 degrees.

When 4/31 Infantry was held up by resistance and casualties north of Hiep Duc, 3/21 Infantry was injected into the grinding fight on its east, in the area known as AK Valley. Over five days of deadly fighting, the 3/21 Infantry rifle companies were ground down by heat, thirst, and the need for relentless contact with the enemy. The command and control helicopter being used by the commander of 3/21 Infantry, Lt. Col. E. P. Howard, was blasted out of the sky by NVA 12.7mm machine guns. Colonel Howard, his sergeant major, and his radio operator and the helicopter crew were killed. Other helicopters were shot down. Resupply of ammunition, food, and water was erratic at best. Eventually the 3d NVA Regiment withdrew slowly to the mountains to rebuild.

In one instance the exhausted survivors of Company A, 3/21, balked at an order. Battalion firebase ordered the company to attack a group of bunkers thought to be abandoned, and recover the bodies of two Americans. When the men balked the battalion executive officer and sergeant major flew to the company and led the men forward. Their company commander, a junior lieutenant and new in combat, was relieved and a more experienced captain was placed in command.

The incident was minor and temporary. The press played it as an "antiwar revolt." It was not. It was the product of several factors, such as experienced leaders being killed and wounded, days of endless combat, heat, thirst, hunger, and frustration. Most of all, it reflected a shift in attitude among the infantry, a resentment that orders came over the radio from senior officers far away who did not join them to take the risks they were taking. And in the words of one captain, there was resentment when the senior officer was not there "to explain why such and such a hill was worth taking—especially when they'd already taken it twice before and walked away from it as soon as the battle was over."

Ho Chi Minh, "Uncle Ho," died in Hanoi in the first week of September, to be replaced by a committee. On 11 September, 60th MF VC battalion assaulted LZ Siberia just across the Song Thu Bon River from Hiep Duc. Troops of 4/31 Infantry drove them off with heavy casualties.

For the rest of 1969, no major battles were fought in the 196th AO. Col. James B. Lee succeeded Colonel Tackaberry in command of the 196th in November.

HISTORY SESSION: A captain, the 196th Light Inf Bd's official historian, conducts an after-combat interview with men of Co A, 3d Bn, 21st Inf. Although 3/21 had won a valorous unit citation, A/3/21 received more notoriety for balking at an order, which led to their company commander being relieved.

Heavy load

Firebases and Vietnam- ization

"VIETNAMIZATION" took hold at the beginning of 1970. US military strength in Vietnam totalled 475,200, but major US combat units such as the 9th Infantry Division and 3d Marine Division had gone home. In January, Henry Kissinger began secret peace talks in Paris.

In the northern provinces, the situation was deceptively quiet, made more so by the beauty of the landscape. But fine young men still died or were maimed by booby traps, land mines blew up trucks, and ground fire peppered helicopters.

Although the war might appear quiet, Greg Cook, who served in Company C, 2/1 Infantry, in 1969–70, said: "The price of being a grunt was getting higher. On 16 March a booby trap series, a daisy chain, cost our company 17 casualties. On 28 March, a 'Bouncing Betty' mine took out my seven-man squad."

Cook called the infantryman's load "the eternally cursed rucksack." The rucksack, he said, "provided us the means to transport all our worldly possessions, field gear, water (three or four canteens full), food, and ammo. Ammo ranging from bullets and grenades to extras: ammo for the machine gun, claymore mines, mortar or recoilless rifle rounds, and C-4 plastic explosive. The load in hot weather and airless valleys caused many a heat casualty."

In this time of steady small-scale contacts, Colonel Jim Lee's tour in command of the 196th was up. Col. Edwin Kennedy succeeded him in April.

LZ Siberia, the firebase closest to Hiep Duc, was again the target of NVA attacks in May and June. Manned by 4/31 Infantry, Siberia was a strong position and was well covered by artillery fires from FSB West, five miles away. ("Siberia" referred to service by the 31st Infantry in 1919 in Russia.) 1st

Medal of Honor —Sgt. Robert C. Murray, posthumously awarded the Medal of Honor for his gallantry when he threw himself on a grenade that was accidentally tripped by a member of his squad.

VC MF Regiment opened the offensive. The firebase was manned by Company D, 4/31 Infantry, and Battery C, 3/82 Artillery, who beat off the attack.

Robert Murray, a 23-year-old staff sergeant in B/4/31, earned the Medal of Honor on 7 June. As a squad leader, he was leading his men in searching for an enemy mortar. One of Murray's men tripped a booby trap that was a grenade rigged with a trip wire. The soldier realized what he had done and shouted for everyone to take cover. Knowing the danger and with disregard for his own safety, S/Sgt. Murray threw himself on the grenade.

A series of sharp firefights in the lowlands around Hiep Duc led the 196th to commit 2/1 and 3/21 Infantry into the area. Fighting continued for six days before the NVA pulled back into the hills. After a lull of a few days NVA forces returned, in squad and platoon size. Over several weeks, every battalion of the 196th (including 1/46 Infantry and 1/1 Cavalry) made contact. In nearly two months almost 600 NVA troops were killed before the main units melted back into the sanctuary of the mountains.

The endless patrols were helped by the acute senses of scout dogs and tracker dogs. German Shepherd scout dogs and labrador retriever tracker teams had entered service with the 196th in January 1967. Lieutenant John Adams III, a platoon leader of A/2/1, told how Leslie (the handler) and King (the scout dog) performed on one of his patrols. The team warned the patrol about two caves and one tunnel, and found two caches and 18 mines.

In mid-July troops of the 196th returned to Kham Duc, part of Operation Elk Canyon I. ARVN and US battalions flew out to the abandoned Kham Duc camp to assert temporary control over the vicinity. 2/1 Infantry, commanded by Lt. Col. Alton Coleman, was given the mission of being the first US unit back, fitting because 2/1 Infantry troops were the last soldiers out when Kham Duc was overrun on 12 May 1968.

Helicopters lifted 2/1 Infantry into Kham Duc on 12 July. An eerie scene unfolded. NVA forces that overran the place had not policed the battlefield. More than 300 mortar rounds and piles of abandoned equipment littered the place. US and NVA remains were intermingled in the graves.

2/1 Infantry secured the area. ARVN units were

lifted by helicopter into the surrounding hills on short operations as part of the training essential for Vietnamization.

Charlie Company, set up in a strong position atop Hill 492, overlooked Kham Duc airstrip, Highway 14, and approaches from the west and south. It was the knobby ridge from which North Vietnamese AAA gunners gave such trouble to aircraft flying to the evacuation of Kham Duc in May 1968.

Units spent more than six weeks at Kham Duc.

DOG TEAM:
A dog handler runs his dog through a tunnel in training. Dogs frequently uncovered enemy caches.

Heavy load

LZ MARY ANN:
The layout of the heavily defended LZ Mary Ann. Situated 38 miles west of Chu Lai and built on a hilltop formed by two smaller hills with a saddle between them, it was isolated and capable of resupply and reinforcement only by helicopter.

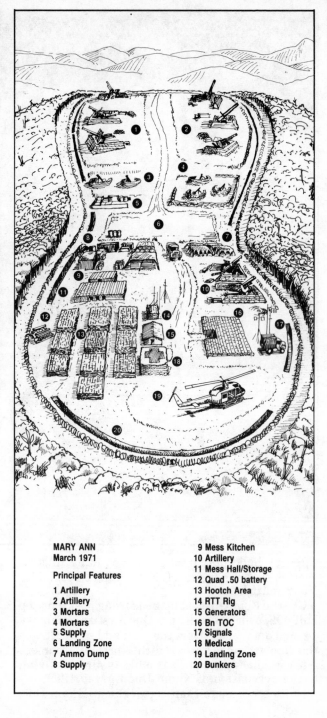

MARY ANN
March 1971

Principal Features

1 Artillery	9 Mess Kitchen
2 Artillery	10 Artillery
3 Mortars	11 Mess Hall/Storage
4 Mortars	12 Quad .50 battery
5 Supply	13 Hootch Area
6 Landing Zone	14 RTT Rig
7 Ammo Dump	15 Generators
8 Supply	16 Bn TOC
	17 Signals
	18 Medical
	19 Landing Zone
	20 Bunkers

Much of the resupply of that far-off base was flown by USAF C-123 Provider aircraft. 196th units left Kham Duc on 25 August.

Meanwhile, other brigade units were building firebases between Kham Duc and the southern border of Quang Tin province. Farthest west was LZ Judy, set up by 2/1 Infantry. Seven miles east toward Chu Lai, 1/46 Infantry built LZ Mary Ann.

These firebases were within 4.2-inch mortar and 105mm artillery range of each other and were mutually supporting. But they were far west of Chu Lai (38 miles for Mary Ann). The one-lane road back toward the coast ended at Hau Duc, five miles east of LZ Mary Ann, on a hilltop formed by two smaller hills with a saddle between them. Resupply and reinforcement was by helicopter.

Montagnard tribesmen had grown corn on the hill, using "slash and burn" to clear the brush. Air strikes of 2,000-pound bombs had cratered it. The troops sought temporary shelter in craters and foxholes. Cubical metal "Conex" shipping containers were airlifted next, settling into the deep craters and making instant operations and signal centers. Infantrymen and men of the supporting arms dug fighting positions, cleared fields of fire, and dug positions for 81mm and 4.2-inch mortars and 105mm artillery howitzers.

Everyone filled sandbags, dug trenches and fighting positions—and sweated in the midsummer heat. Concertina wire was laid around the perimeter. Helicopters sprayed defoliant outside the perimeter; vegetation soon turned brown and died. Engineer demolition parties blasted large trees with C-4 plastic explosive and TNT. Eventually a field kitchen was flown in. As time passed, the men improved the shelters, making them more livable. Shelters were crude, usually built from discarded wooden ammo boxes filled with dirt, supported by metal engineer stakes, and protected all around by walls of sandbags.

When American Division decided to make LZ Mary Ann a permanent base, a CH-47 helicopter lifted in a small bulldozer. Engineers excavated a hole about 30 × 50 feet for the battalion tactical operations center (TOC). With the TOC built, the engineers constructed a mess kitchen and dining hall above ground. Eventually, wooden bunkers about 10 × 10

Sandbag city —Each LZ in the hilltop chain of landing zones established by the 196th west of Chu Lai consisted of heavily protected bunkers and forests of aerial masts. But the protection was no substitute for an alert attitude—as events at LZ Mary Ann proved.

feet were prefabricated at Chu Lai and lifted to Mary Ann to be lowered into prepared holes. The bunkers were sandbagged on top and all around. Three or four men lived in each bunker.

During the construction period, one rifle company of 1/46 provided base security (along with the artillery and others). Other rifle companies patrolled throughout the key region. Andrew Olints was a junior sergeant (E-5) in Company D. After basic training, he was selected for NCO (noncommissioned officer) school at Fort Benning, a method by which the Army made up for its shortage of experienced noncoms. Successful graduates were

promoted to Sergeant E-5. As Olints put it, "A lot of people called us 'Shake and Bakes,' for becoming 'Instant NCOs.'"

Olints joined Company D while it was around Que Son and Hiep Duc. He wondered how the men would accept a "Shake and Bake" sergeant with no combat experience. "Much to my surprise, no one cared about rank. They were just happy to have someone to help them. If you didn't fit into the squad properly, believe me, someone would actually kick your ass. I could not believe how professional the men acted. Each man knew his job and was proud of what he was doing. When you would meet someone, he would

COVER AND POINT:
A point man indicates the source of enemy fire to men. The eyes and ears of a squad, his instincts were critical to their survival.

give his name and then tell you his job, like point man or RTO."

Patrol missions lasted from 5 to 28 days. Olints's first was for 21 days, in the hills west of Mary Ann. The company flew into the patrol base in a combat assault. Its platoons fanned out in different directions to cover large areas. Platoons at that time had 20 to 23 men in three squads. The squads took turns walking point.

Olints remembered the nights. "No one talked at night. We would set out three claymore mines and trip flares. The two M-60 machine guns were set up to cover the trails. All night long we had at least two men awake with PRC-25 radios in their hands. We slept in hammocks, using ponchos for overhead cover."

"Every day in the bush was exciting. We did not have contacts every day, but there was always something different. In the mountains we would move about one kilometer (5/8 of a mile) a day. With the hills, rivers, old Montagnard villages, pigs, chickens, digging up NVA graves, finding NVA base camps, the heat, and wet weather, we were busy all day."

No major battles were fought in the rest of 1970. NVA and VC troops ranged about the area in small squad-sized groups. Units of the 196th set ambushes and patrolled to detect the movement, take prisoners, and make enemy concentrations more difficult.

In later November and early December, 1/46 Infantry had heavy contacts with NVA units around Tien Phuoc. Andy Olints recalled the briefing before

FACTORY FIND:
Men of Co C, 4th Bn, 31st Inf, with material and a sampan found at an NVA factory where boats up to 14 feet were built.

Cost-effective —An infantryman listens for a signal on his portable metal detector while minesweeping a road. Shortly after the brigade's arrival in Vietnam the decision was taken to buy civilian metal detectors, of the type used by treasure hunters, to supplement conventional Army issue. Despite the doubts of the manufacturer as to suitability, the detectors were a success and were used throughout the 196th's stay in Vietnam.

his company made a combat assault. "When they said, 'Take extra ammo,' we knew we were in trouble. November meant monsoon season and wet cold. On the combat assault, one of the Kit Carson scouts (Vietnamese) got out of the chopper and then jumped back in. No way would he work the area!"

Patrols found plenty of evidence of the NVA out in the hills. In early February 1971, Charlie Company was patrolling far west of the base when its point man spotted a hootch. He walked into the hut and found more than 500 weapons stacked in it: AK-47 assault rifles, machine guns, rockets. Andrew Olints's company was lifted out the next morning to replace Charlie Company on patrol. For the next 16 days, Company D was in steady contact. They found an NVA base camp where boats up to 14 feet were built.

In early 1971 Company E, 1/46, on patrol south of the base, found 102mm ChiCom rockets aimed at Mary Ann: clear evidence of an impending attack.

Andrew Olints and other soldiers of 1/46 were suspicious of the 20 or so ARVN troops manning the two 105mm howitzers at the base. They suspected the ARVN troops might be leaving information for NVA units at the water point down the hill, or even sneaking NVA scouts onto the firebase.

As part of the US troop withdrawal, Mary Ann was to be abandoned. LZ Mildred at Hau Duc, a few miles east, was reactivated in early March. Mildred could be resupplied over the road from Tam Ky if necessary; Mary Ann could not. When LZ Mildred was fully functional the whole setup would be turned over to ARVN units.

Mortars from 1/46 were shifted from Mary Ann to Mildred, and Company A manned it. Gary Noller, was on Mary Ann until midafternoon on 27 March, then went over to his company at Mildred. On the night of 27-28 March Company A was at Mildred and Company C on Mary Ann. Main weapons on LZ Mary Ann were two US 155mm howitzers and two ARVN 105mm howitzers. Total strength was 251 US and 20 ARVN soldiers. Companies B and D were patrolling in the field Gary Noller remembered.

Enemy sappers attacked LZ Mary Ann at 0230 on 28 March. Heavy fire from 82mm mortars started the attack. The 8.6-pound teardrop shaped rounds whistled down, exploding with a *kaboom* sound and

Heavy load

UNDER DIFFERENT FLAGS:
Men of the 196th display a Soviet flag (top) captured during a search-and-destroy mission. Earlier patrols had reported seeing six-foot-tall Caucasian advisors at NVA base camps. An ARVN officer (bottom) places a streamer on a 1st Sqn, 1st Cav, 196th Light Inf Bde, flagstaff in February 1971. As "Vietnam-ization," increased so did the number of handing-over flag ceremonies.

Gen Creighton W. Abrams —Headed the investigation into the disaster at LZ Mary Ann.

spraying thousands of curled steel fragments low to the ground. Sappers followed the mortar barrage with hand grenades and B-40 rockets. Sweeping from south to north, they emplaced satchel charges to blow up friendly fortifications.

The sappers homed in on the Tactical Operation Center, destroying it and obliterating the control of units on the firebase. The attack lasted less than 30 minutes. All US-fortified bunkers were destroyed. The ARVN bunker was untouched.

By 0300, the sappers withdrew, leaving the base devastated and demoralized: 30 US soldiers were killed; 82 were wounded. Enemy casualties were 5 to 15 killed.

The officers and troops of 1/46 Infantry on LZ Mary Ann were victims of complacency. There had been no enemy action against the remote base for months. On the night of the attack, senior investigating officers believed the troops were not alert, a clear failing of officer supervision.

General Westmoreland, the Army chief of staff, asked General Abrams to investigate.

General Abrams concluded that the Americal Division commander, Maj. Gen. James L. Baldwin, was unaware of the lackluster defenses at Mary Ann. Baldwin visited the base frequently, but apparently did not probe its defenses. General Baldwin was relieved. Also relieved were the 196th brigade and 1/46 battalion commanders, Col. William S. Hathaway and Lt. Col. W. B. Doyle. Abrams concluded that they did not carry out their responsibilities for ensuring that the troops were prepared and alert and that the basic defense plan was followed.

LZs Mary Ann and Mildred were soon abandoned. 1/46 Infantry moved to Da Nang with the 196th headquarters, to protect the port installations as the American withdrawal accelerated. The brigade's 2/1 Infantry was already dispatched far to the north. From 1 March to 8 April it operated between Dong Ha and the DMZ to provide security for areas vacated by ARVN units, on the expedition into Laos called Operation Lam Son 719. When it ended on 6 April, 2/1 Infantry returned to the brigade. The 196th now was responsible for an area encompassing almost 1,200 square miles, about the size of Rhode Island.

Heavy load

THE VISIT:

Lt. Col. William P. Doyle of the 1st Bn, 46th Inf, demonstrates a captured NVA rifle to Maj. Gen. James L. Baldwin during a visit to LZ Mary Ann on 4 February 1971. Nearly two months later Mary Ann was overrun by NVA sappers, who killed 30 US servicemen and wounded 82. Both Baldwin and Doyle and another commander were relieved of their commands for failing to ensure that the troops were prepared and alert.

Final shots

9

Contraction and shutdown

GENERAL CREIGHTON ABRAMS sent Maj. Gen. Frederick J. Kroesen back to Chu Lai to take command of the Americal Division in July 1971. Kroesen found to his pleasure and pride that the community of Hiep Duc was still thriving in the Que Son Valley, despite repeated attempts by NVA and VC forces to drive the people back into refugee camps.

He also found the RF/PF forces more effective, and 2d ARVN Division far more effective than two years earlier, when it "could do little other than defend its own installations." Now its regiments got out into the field with Americal units.

US unit dispositions at Chu Lai were about as two years earlier. The 11th and 198th Brigades were operating from the same firebases around Chu Lai and along Highway 1 in Quang Ngai to the south. The 196th had replaced 1st Marine Division in Quang Nam and was active from Tam Ky all the way up to Da Nang and from the coast out to Hiep Duc and An Hoa in the west. Colonel Rutland Beard had succeeded Col. William Hathaway in command of the 196th in June.

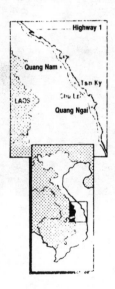

Kroesen decided the combat power of the 198th and 11th Brigades could be better used in an active and dynamic defense. Operations of the 2d ARVN Division and its area of responsibility were already integrated with the Americal. It would take over the remaining bases when Americal's units left. Their departure was imminent.

The first major step was to cut the Chu Lai base force to two battalions, and have 2d ARVN Div take over the area south of Chu Lai. An ARVN regiment would be augmented with US artillery, aviation, and an infantry battalion—good leavening, and a useful

confidence builder for ARVN leaders. XXIV Corps
added two battalions of the 101st Airborne Division
to America's control, augmenting the 196th in
Quang Nam province around Da Nang. The brigade
in early September also had these fighting units: 2/1
Infantry, 3/21 Infantry, 4/31 Infantry, 1/46 Infantry,
1/1 Cavalry, F/17 Cavalry, F/8 Cavalry (Air cavalry
troop), 51st ARVN Regiment, a company of US
Rangers, and various ARVN Rangers, 3/82
Artillery, plus engineer, medical, military police,
ordnance, signal, and other supporting units.

Situation reports showed units continuing to
operate in platoon and company search missions.
Although contacts were infrequent, bullets and

booby traps killed as effectively as always. In July and August the brigade lost 27 soldiers killed and 133 wounded. September and October were quieter, with 7 killed and 8 wounded.

The biggest change, compared with 1969, was drug abuse among US troops, reflecting rising drug incidence in the United States, cheaper prices in Vietnam, and easy availability. In 1968 and 1969, marijuana use increased. In 1970 use of heroin drew even with marijuana in the Americal Division. By January 1971 statistics for heroin use were higher than marijuana.

Men in the rifle companies had their own code for drugs. A stoned GI was a hazard to his buddies and

TAKE YOUR POSITIONS:
A platoon sergeant of 3d Bn, 21st Inf, gives his men last-minute instructions before moving out. Right until the last the 196th stayed on alert.

153

Diversions —Entertainer Bob Hope and Miss World put on a Christmas show at the Americal Division base at Chu Lai. Throughout the stay of the division and the 196th's stay, there was time to be entertained by celebrities and to entertain visiting senators and members of Congress.

was not tolerated in the bush. On the firebases and at Chu Lai, the code relaxed.

Drug use exacerbated and highlighted the hazardous schism between the young soldiers and the senior noncoms and officers ("lifers"). Both may have reflected the situation at home—the drug society and "not trusting anyone over 30." But both influences sapped combat potential.

The first Americal infantry brigade to leave was the 11th Brigade, which stood down on 5 October. The same day, the 4/31 Infantry, the Polar Bears, departed for home. "Grunt of the Month" in the 4/31 was Specialist 4th Class Daniel Van Huss. He read to General Kroesen the battalion's farewell note to the Americal Division. Van Huss quoted President Teddy Roosevelt: "It's not the critic that counts, the credit belongs to the man who is actually in the arena, whose face is marred by dust and sweat and blood. . . ." He said that described soldiers of the Americal Division, then continued:

"If anyone said that he enjoyed being over here we would look at him with a great deal of concern. But if someone said that he did his job, had a good attitude, beat the bush, and indicated he did this because he loved his country—then that is a Polar Bear. If you need us again, we'll come charging. Good luck to all of you and God bless you."

For the remainder of October, men and units of the Americal continued to depart. More soldiers of 2d ARVN Division took over buildings on the huge Chu Lai base.

On 11 November the division and 198th Brigade stood down. The next day in Washington, President Nixon announced that American troops would no longer participate in offensive operations.

The 196th Light Infantry Brigade remained, based at Da Nang. Brig. Gen. Joseph C. McDonough, formerly one of the assistant division commanders of the Americal, took command. The Charger Brigade continued to defend the shrinking American force in the north.

The 2d NVA Division came out of the mountains in January 1972 to retake Hiep Duc. No one was left to stop them, and Hiep Duc was lost. Worse was to come.

North Vietnamese forces smashed across the DMZ at the end of March in an offensive aimed at Kontum

LAST MEN OUT:
Men of Co D, 3d
Bn, 21st Inf,
search for
weapons caches
east of Hill 510
in Quang Tin
province. In
August 1972
3/21 finally
stood down and
became the last
US ground
combat unit to
leave Vietnam.

and Saigon. Quang Tri fell on 1 May. Units of the
196th were sent to Phu Bai as defenders. After
heavy losses inside Vietnam and from massive air
strikes against Hanoi and other targets in North
Vietnam, the offensive abated and the invasion force
withdrew.

1/46 Infantry stood down in June, leaving the
196th with two infantry battalions. Finally, on 29
June the 196th Light Infantry Brigade stood down
after nearly six years of combat. Its 3d Battalion,
21st Infantry (Gimlets), remained two months
longer. The Gimlets left on 23 August, the last
American ground combat unit to leave Vietnam.

For the 196th Light Infantry Brigade the war was
over.

A-4	— McDonnell Douglas Skyhawk attack bomber.
A-6	— Grumman attack plane.
AAA	— Antiaircraft artillery.
AK-47	— Soviet 7.62mm automatic assault rifle (Kalashnikov).
AO	— Area of operations.
ARVN	— Army of the Republic of Vietnam.
B-52	— Boeing Stratofortress heavy bomber.
Battery	— Artillery unit equivalent to infantry company.
Bde	— Brigade.
Bn	— Battalion.
Bunker	— Fighting position with overhead cover.
C-130	— Lockheed Hercules aircraft.
C-123	— Fairchild Provider air transport.
CCT	— Command and control team.
CH-47	— Boeing Chinook transport helicopter.
Charlie	— Nickname for the Viet Cong.
Chicom	— Chinese Communist.
CIDG	— Civilian irregular defense group.
Claymore	— Command-detonated antipersonnel mine.
Co	— Company.
CO	— Commanding officer.
Cobra	— Attack helicopter AH-1G.
Concertina	— Coiled barbed wire used in defensive positions.
COSVN	— The Vietnamese Communist headquarters.
C-rations	— Standard-issue field rations.
DMZ	— Demilitarized Zone.
DRV	— Democratic Republic of Vietnam (North Vietnam).
Dustoff	— Helicopter extraction, usually medical.
F-4	— McDonnell Douglas Phantom attack fighter.
FAC	— Forward air controller.
Flak	— Antiaircraft shrapnel fragments.
FO	— Forward observer.

FSB	— Fire support base.
Greenseed	— New arrival.
Gunship	— Armed helicopter; UH-1 Huey first, later the AH-1 Cobra.
HE	— High explosive.
Huey	— UH-1 utility helicopter.
LZ	— Landing zone.
LRRP	— Long-range reconnaissance patrol.
LZ	— Landing zone.
M-16	— Automatic 5.56mm rifle.
M-48	— Medium tank.
M-60	— 7.62mm machine gun.
M-79	— Grenade launcher.
M-113	— Armored personnel carrier.
MACV	— Military Assistance Command, Vietnam.
MAF	— Marine Amphibious Force.
Napalm	— Incendiary used both as a defoliant and antipersonnel weapon.
NCO	— Noncommissioned officer.
NVA	— North Vietnamese Army.
PF	— Popular Forces.
PFC	— Private first class.
RF	— Regional forces.
RPG	— Rocket-propelled grenade.
RTO	— Radio-telephone operator.
Sapper	— NVA or VC trained in demolitions.
Skyhawk	— A-4 attack aircraft.
Sortie	— Operational flight by a single aircraft.
Spectre	— AC-130 gunship.
Spooky	— AC-47 gunship.
Task Force (TF)	— Temporary grouping of units for a specific task.
Tet	— Vietnamese lunar New Year.
USARV	— US Army Vietnam.
USMC	— US Marine Corps.
VC	— Viet Cong.
Vietnamization	— Handing the war over to the South Vietnamese.
WHA	— Wounded by hostile action.

About
the Author

F. Clifton Berry, Jr.

F. Clifton Berry, Jr., was a paratrooper and airborne infantry officer in the 82d Airborne Division. He saw Vietnam combat as operations officer of the 196th Light Infantry Brigade, logging 600 flying hours in helicopters and FAC aircraft.

In an Army career, he commanded airborne and infantry units from squad through battalion level in the US and Far East.

Following active service, since 1975 he has been an editor and writer on military and aerospace topics. He was co-editor of *Armed Forces Journal*, editor in chief of *AIR FORCE Magazine*, and chief US editor of the Interavia publishing group. He is the author of *Sky Soldiers* and *Strike Aircraft*, volumes in the Illustrated History of the Vietnam War series.

He is a master parachutist and active pilot, with land and seaplane ratings.

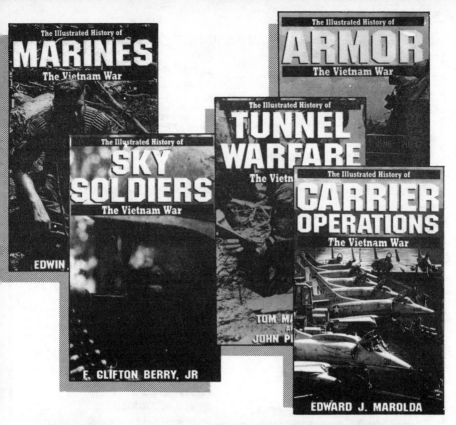

THE ILLUSTRATED HISTORY OF THE VIETNAM WAR

antam's Illustrated History of the Vietnam War is a unique and new series of books exploring in depth the war that seared America to the core: a war that cost 58,186 American lives, that saw great heroism and resourcefulness mixed with terrible destruction and tragedy.

The Illustrated History of the Vietnam War examines exactly what happened. Every significant aspect—the physical details, the operations, and the strategies behind them—is analyzed in short, crisply written original books by established historians and journalists.

Some books are devoted to key battles and campaigns, others unfold the stories of elite groups and fighting units, while others focus on the role of specific weapons and tactics.

Each volume is totally original and is richly illustrated with photographs, line drawings, and maps.